FOR TIMES
OF TROUBLE

FOR TIMES
OF TROUBLE

◆ SPIRITUAL SOLACE FROM THE PSALMS ◆

JEFFREY R. HOLLAND

**DESERET
BOOK**

SALT LAKE CITY, UTAH

Library of Congress Cataloging-in-Publication Data

Holland, Jeffrey R., author.
  For times of trouble : spiritual solace from the Psalms / Jeffrey R. Holland.
    pages   cm
  Includes bibliographical references and index.
  ISBN 978-1-60907-271-1 (hardbound : alk. paper)
1. Bible. O.T. Psalms—Meditations.   2. Consolation.   3. Christian life—Mormon authors.   4. The Church of Jesus Christ of Latter-day Saints—Doctrines.   5. Mormon Church—Doctrines.   I. Title.
  BS1430.54.H65 2012
  223'.1077—dc23   2012033592

Printed in the United States of America
Publishers Printing, Salt Lake City, UT

10   9   8   7   6   5   4   3   2   1

FOR PAT

We took sweet counsel together,
and walked unto the house of God in company.

PSALM 55:14

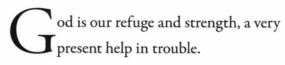

God is our refuge and strength, a very present help in trouble.

Therefore will not we fear, though the earth be removed, and though the mountains be carried into the midst of the sea;

Though the waters thereof roar and be troubled, though the mountains shake with the swelling thereof. . . .

The Lord . . . will be a refuge for the oppressed, a refuge in times of trouble.

PSALMS 46:1–3; 9:9

CONTENTS

Preface xi

SECTION 1: REFLECTIONS

"The Troubles of
My Heart" 3

Psalm 56:9 12

Psalm 1:1–3. 15

Psalm 3:2–5 18

Psalm 4:1 20

Psalms 4:4; 27:14;
46:10 22

Psalm 4:6–7 25

Psalms 5:1; 119:15, 48 . . . 27

Psalm 5:11–12 30

Psalms 6:2–4, 6, 8; 57:1 . . 32

Psalm 8:2 35

Psalm 11:1 37

Psalms 15:1–3; 17:3;
34:13 39

Psalm 17:8 42

Psalms 18:2, 30; 61:2;
62:6 43

Psalms 18:36;
94:18–19 45

Psalms 19:1–3; 8:3–6 . . . 47

Psalm 19:13 51

Psalm 20:7 53

Psalm 22:4–5 55

Psalms 24:3–4; 51:10 57

Psalm 25:7 60

Psalm 27:4–5 62

CONTENTS

Psalm 27:10 64

Psalms 30:5; 42:5;
    130:6 66

Psalms 31:12; 34:18;
    51:10, 17 69

Psalm 32:7 71

Psalm 34:7 73

Psalm 36:9 76

Psalms 37:16; 49:16–17;
    73:3 78

Psalm 37:23–24 82

Psalm 40:10 84

Psalm 41:1 86

Psalm 55:16–17 90

Psalms 57:7; 26:1–2, 11 . . . 93

Psalm 61:2 95

Psalm 69:3 97

Psalm 71:9, 18 99

Psalm 77:10–12 101

Psalms 78:5–8; 145:4 103

Psalm 85:11 106

Psalms 86:3–6; 103:8–11,
    17–18; 119:58 108

Psalm 89:9 111

Psalm 89:30–34 113

Psalms 94:9–10; 100:3, 5;
    119:99–100 115

Psalm 105:15 117

Psalm 113:9 119

Psalm 116:15 121

Psalm 118:6 123

Psalm 118:24 125

Psalm 119:19 127

Psalm 119:59–60 129

Psalm 119:67, 71–72 131

Psalm 119:94 133

Psalms 119:103, 105;
    12:6; 18:28 134

Psalm 119:108 137

Psalm 127:1 139

Psalm 127:3–5 141

Psalm 133:1 143

Psalm 139:23 145

Psalm 141:3 147

Psalm 141:5 149

Psalm 144:12 150

Psalms 145:14; 146:8 152

CONTENTS

SECTION 2: THE MESSIAH

Some Messianic
Psalms 157

Psalm 2 159

Psalm 8 162

Psalm 16 165

Psalm 21 169

Psalm 45 171

Psalm 68 173

Psalm 72 176

Psalm 89 179

Psalm 102 181

Psalm 110 184

Psalm 118 187

Crucifixion and
Atonement 192

**SECTION 3:
THE TWENTY-THIRD PSALM**

Psalm 23 201

Green Pastures, Still
Waters, and the
Good Shepherd . . . 202

Notes 227

Scripture Index 233

Subject Index 239

PREFACE

What the reader will find in this book are personal musings and private meditations on a very eclectic selection of the psalms. In fact, only rarely do I include a psalm in its entirety; for the most part there is commentary on a line here and a line there, or perhaps on a cluster of verses pulled together from several psalms. Furthermore, there is little here reflecting the insights of scholars who know the language, culture, and history of the Old Testament period from which these psalms come. I have occasionally included a thought or citation from someone else, but very infrequently. Because the book is more devotional in nature than comprehensive in its commentary, I have not included some elements of doctrine that a more thorough treatment would likely address—for example, I have not focused on material from the Joseph Smith Translation of the Bible or on passages that may be used liturgically in other religions.

Because these entries are primarily meditations, they are my thoughts alone and as such are not the only—much less the best—thoughts one could put in such a book. The personal nature of these essays should make it clear that this collection is not an official publication of The Church of Jesus Christ of Latter-day Saints. I alone am responsible for the teachings here. If there are errors of judgment, analysis, or insight, they are mine and no one else's.

A word or two about the authorship of the psalms is also relevant in this preface. These poems/songs/prayers are traditionally attributed to David, the boy shepherd who would become the most popular king in ancient Israel's history. However, it is almost certain that David did *not* write all of the psalms collected in the Bible. Contemporary scholars do not agree and cannot know for certain about such matters, but it is enough to know that David wrote many of the psalms, and perhaps even most of them. Fortunately for the purposes of this book, authorship of any given psalm is not a major issue one way or the other. To sidestep that entire controversy I simply refer throughout this work to "the Psalmist."

The selections I have chosen are roughly sequential, starting from the first and working to the conclusion of the collection as it now appears in the Bible. However, the sequence of these pieces has no particular relevance. For example, I began with Psalm 56 as something of an introduction to all that follows simply because I felt it was the right message with which to start the book. Furthermore, I have freely clustered various passages from multiple psalms in whatever way seemed to reflect a relationship or similarity of ideas.

As always, I wish to thank my devoted secretary of more than a quarter century, Randi Greene. She typed the diverse elements of this manuscript when they came in as bits and pieces, always being unfailingly positive about fragmented thoughts and minor literary bursts that could not have made much sense to her when they appeared on her desk. I am sad to note that by the time this book is published, Randi will have retired from our employment. Everyone in my family and in our office will miss her dearly.

My thanks, too, for the professionalism and personal encouragement of my friends at Deseret Book Company, especially Sheri Dew,

Cory Maxwell, Emily Watts, Richard Erickson, and, on this particular book, Lisa Roper and Allison Mathews. They have suffered with more chaos, more starts and stops, and more missed deadlines than any editors and publishers deserve, but they have smiled through it all and kept any real grousing out of earshot.

Finally, I thank my wife, Pat, who wonders why I conceive such projects but lovingly supports me in the pursuit of them. Much of the time spent on this book was time taken from her, but, as always, she never expressed a single complaint nor lamented through those late nights when the light was still on. It would take someone with the talent of a psalmist to capture in verse her splendor. This book is dedicated to her.

JEFFREY R. HOLLAND
Salt Lake City, Utah
2012

SECTION 1
REFLECTIONS

"THE TROUBLES OF MY HEART"

One of the unfailing facts of mortal life is the recurring presence of trouble, the recurring challenge of difficulty and pain. So often we find ourselves swimming against the tide in what Hamlet called "a sea of troubles."[1] Someone once reasoned that confronting problems is apparently the common denominator of the living—the great bond between the rich and the poor, the learned and the ignorant, the believer and the skeptic. It is very clear that anyone, including the righteous, who enters the chaotic currents of life is going to face trials and tribulations along the way. One popular writer said that expecting a trouble-free life because you are a good person is like expecting the bull not to charge you because you are a vegetarian.[2]

When these difficult days (and nights!) come—and they will—it will help us to remember that "it must needs be," that in the grand councils of heaven before the world was, we agreed to such a time of challenge and refinement. We were taught then that facing, resolving, and enduring troublesome times was the price we would pay for progress. And we were committed to progress eternally. In a great patriarchal pronouncement given nearly three millennia ago, the prophet

3

Lehi taught that it was fundamental to God's eternal plan that our quest for exaltation—the triumph of righteousness over wickedness, of happiness over misery, of good over evil—requires "opposition in all things."[3] Thus, even though on some days we might wish it otherwise, it is essential that our temporal journey be laced with all kinds of choices and alternatives, opportunities and obstacles, exhilarating highs and sometimes devastating lows. Through addressing—and occasionally simply enduring—these myriad experiences we are to learn and improve, grow and repent, have faith, keep trying, and make our way toward our eternal home.

Of course, the greatest reassurance in this plan is that there was from the beginning a fail-safe protection built into the arrangement, an unassailable guarantee (if we want it) against every mistake we might make, every sin we would commit, every trial we would confront, every discouragement, disease, and the death we will all ultimately face. This salvation would come in the form of a Messiah, *the* Messiah—the Lord Jesus Christ, the Son of God. He would come "with healing in his wings,"[4] both temporally and spiritually. His message would be one of hope and peace. His atoning sacrifice would overcome death and hell for every man, woman, and child from Adam to the end of the world. He would break the bands of our bondage and our troubles, and He would set us free. But more about that later.

Though we have received great promises regarding the lifting of our burdens, the weight of them is still often ponderous while we wait for that relief. It was for just such days of opposition, such "times of trouble," that a large percentage of the biblical psalms were written. Consider these pleading passages:

> *Be not far from me; for trouble is near; for there is none to help.*[5]

Or this:

Turn thee unto me, and have mercy upon me; for I am desolate and afflicted.

The troubles of my heart are enlarged: O bring thou me out of my distresses.

Look upon mine affliction and my pain; and forgive all my sins.[6]

Or this:

Save me, O God; for the waters are come in unto my soul.

I sink in deep mire, where there is no standing: I am come into deep waters, where the floods overflow me.

I am weary of my crying: my throat is dried: mine eyes fail while I wait for my God. . . .

Deliver me out of the mire, and let me not sink: let me be delivered from them that hate me, and out of the deep waters.

Let not the waterflood overflow me, neither let the deep swallow me up, and let not the pit shut her mouth upon me.

Hear me, O Lord; for thy lovingkindness is good: turn unto me according to the multitude of thy tender mercies.

And hide not thy face from thy servant; for I am in trouble: hear me speedily.[7]

Or this:

They mount up to the heaven, they go down again to the depths: their soul is melted because of trouble.

They reel to and fro, and stagger like a drunken man, and are at their wits' end.

Then they cry unto the Lord in their trouble, and he bringeth them out of their distresses.

He maketh the storm a calm, so that the waves thereof are still.

Then are they glad because they be quiet; so he bringeth them unto their desired haven.

Oh that men would praise the Lord for his goodness, and for his wonderful works to the children of men![8]

These and so many other passages like them become the spiritual equivalent of what a fierce combatant declared in the days of political and religious revolution that set the stage for the Restoration of the gospel. Paraphrasing the defiant Thomas Paine, I, too, "love those who can smile in trouble, who can gather strength from distress, and grow brave by reflection. It is the business of little minds to shrink, but they whose heart is firm, and whose conscience approves their conduct, will pursue their principles unto death."[9]

The primary purpose of these scriptural psalms is to help us "grow brave by reflection," help us exert the faith necessary to "smile in trouble" and "gather strength from distress." The promises of light to those who are engulfed in darkness and strength for those who are battling an enemy are regularly recurring themes throughout the psalms.

These near-constant pleas to God in time of danger and cries to heaven for comfort amidst chaos are not the only themes running through the psalms, but they constitute a significant portion of these ancient songs that are prayers and prayers that are songs. Even acknowledging the other poetic topics addressed in this greatest of all devotional literature, it is revealing to note how many of those are supplementary to this primary theme. There are many other kinds of psalms—scholars suggest as many as seven classifications or "genres" for the psalms—filled with such topics as peace and praise, nature and nationalism, zeal and the quest for Zion.

6

But the backdrop behind even these more wide-ranging reflections is the realization that life is very difficult and mortals need God's constant care in order to prevail. The psalms classified as "supplications"—prayers or pleadings for God's help and protection in times of distress—outnumber the psalms within any other genre by a wide margin.

It has been asserted that the book of Psalms as a whole has exerted more influence on the Western world than any other collection of poetic verse ever written.[10] Whether or not that is true may be a matter of literary opinion, but surely it *is* true that for Bible readers generally, the Psalms have been among the most personally applicable and most privately embraced scriptures in the entire canon. In that canon, this book is unique in its intense longing for deliverance, solace, and safety. It does not document history in the way much of the Old Testament does, nor does it focus on the ministries or doctrinal writings of prophetic figures. Furthermore, other collections of "wisdom literature," such as Proverbs, Ecclesiastes, and the Song of Solomon, are included in the Bible alongside Psalms. But none of these others—combined!—compare with the personal tone, content, quantity, and quality of the psalms, these pleas to a compassionate God, to the healer of broken hearts, to the Savior of the downtrodden and destitute. As such, the book of Psalms may be the one biblical text admired nearly equally by both Christians and Jews, to say nothing of those of other faiths—or no faith at all—who find comfort in its verses and encouragement in the hope they convey.

In this sense the psalms are something of a biblical bridge reaching to all people, most particularly to those traveling back and forth between the Old and New Testaments. Of a total of 283 direct citations from the Old Testament contained in the New, 116 are identified as coming from Psalms. Jesus Himself quoted the book of Psalms more than any other Old Testament text. Beyond the Savior's own use of these writings, the authors of the four Gospels drew heavily on the psalms as they strove to document His life and ministry, particularly those excruciating hours of His arrest, trial, and Crucifixion. It could be argued that in all of holy writ, no book of scripture goes on so extensively about the Messianic mission or the looking and longing for His return that is expressed in the songs of the Psalmist. Certainly, nothing so elevated the status of the psalms in this regard as did Jesus' own words to His disciples after His Resurrection and before His ascension. After appearing to them, showing them His resurrected body, and eating fish and honeycomb with them, "He said unto them, These are the words which I spake unto you, while I was yet with you, that all things must be fulfilled, which were written in the law of Moses, and in the prophets, *and in the psalms,* concerning me. Then opened he their understanding, that they might understand the scriptures."[11] In terms of Messianic message and insight into the great Jehovah—past, present, and future—the book of Psalms here takes its rightful place with the highly esteemed and much more frequently acknowledged "law and the prophets."[12]

As something of a conclusion to this introductory chapter, it may be of interest to the reader to note two other connections between the psalms and the gospel of Jesus Christ. First it should be understood that a significant number of the psalms were composed for use in the temple, or at the very least were incorporated into the temple experience because of their beauty and doctrinal relevance. Entire volumes of scholarly commentary have been devoted to the consideration of these "temple psalms." It is not the purpose of this book to pursue that topic, but suffice it to say that when the ancient Israelites heard certain of these prayerful texts, they would have immediately associated them with the temple. It is not surprising that such encouraging doctrine would be linked with a temple experience that was meant to be as comforting anciently as it is today. When any of us are distressed or discouraged or needing special guidance, we go to the temple. Both then and now the children of Israel could turn to the psalms as being part of—and reminiscent of—that experience.

That leads to the second link to be noted, which is that the Sermon on the Mount generally—and the introductory verses known as the Beatitudes in particular—reflect both the teachings of the psalms and the temple experience.[13] Rather than pursue this Sermon on the Mount/temple relationship in detail, let me use just two examples from the Beatitudes to make the point.

Biblical scholars have noted that in the Old Testament texts, the word *blessed* (*'ashre* in Hebrew) is used to introduce a verse more than forty times. At least twenty-six of those examples are in the book of Psalms. Indeed it is not coincidental that the very first psalm begins "*Blessed* is the man . . ."[14]

With this phrasing so familiar to those who loved the psalms, and with Jesus having gone up "into a mountain"[15] just as Israelites went up "to the mountain of the Lord, to the house of the God of Jacob,"[16] the beatitude/temple/psalms connection is as firm as it is intentional.

Then, on the mountain (of Beatitudes), Jesus taught, "Blessed are the pure in heart: for they shall see God."[17] It can be safely assumed the Savior knew that His listeners, when hearing those words, would remember Psalm 24, one of the "psalms of ascent" sung by both priest and layman who "went up" to the temple to worship God and—someday—to see Him. The link between purity of heart and the privilege of beholding the face of the Lord is quite clear in the King James Version but even more explicit in the Septuagint (LXX).[18] Both are noted here for comparison:

Who shall ascend into the hill of the Lord? or who shall stand in his holy place?

He that hath clean hands, and a pure heart; who hath not lifted up his soul unto vanity, nor sworn deceitfully.

He shall receive the blessing from the Lord, and righteousness from the God of his salvation.

This is the generation of them that seek him, that seek thy face, O Jacob. . . .

Who is this King of glory? The Lord of hosts, he is the King of glory.

(Psalm 24:3–6, 10, KJV)

Who shall go up to the mountain of the Lord, and who shall stand in his holy place? He that is innocent in his hands and pure in his heart; who has not lifted up his soul to vanity, nor sworn deceitfully to his neighbour. He shall receive a blessing from the Lord, and mercy from God his Saviour. This is the generation of them that seek him, that seek the face of the God of Jacob. . . .

Who is this king of glory? The Lord of hosts, he is this king of glory.

(Psalm 24:3–6, 10, LXX)

This psalm makes it clear that those who go to "the mountain of the Lord" to "stand in his holy place"—the temple—must have clean, innocent hands and a pure heart. Then, and only then, is one entitled to see the face of God. Thus, in one simple sentence—"Blessed are the pure in heart: for they shall see God"—Jesus makes an immediate connection with the psalms, with the temple, and with the Christian discipleship expected of the people He was teaching.[19]

A second, briefer example from the Beatitudes is, "Blessed are the meek: for they shall inherit the earth."[20] This language used by Jesus is taken directly from Psalm 37:11: "But the meek shall inherit the earth; and shall delight themselves in the abundance of peace."

And so it goes with the Beatitudes specifically, the Sermon on the Mount generally, and a host of other teachings common to the Old Testament and the New. With all of this in mind, I invite the reader to consider just a few of the other blessings and promises that

PSALM 107:28–30

Then they cry unto the Lord in their trouble, and he bringeth them out of their distresses.

He maketh the storm a calm, so that the waves thereof are still.

Then are they glad because they be quiet; so he bringeth them unto their desired haven.

the psalms hold for those who, both then and now, cry out for help. In these selections is the repeated promise that the Lord will watch over us in every such moment and heal us from every hurt. Yes, there will be stress and sorrow in life, and we will not always get the answers from heaven we prefer, but God will always give the answer we need—and with it He will give both strength and spiritual solace in all our times of trouble.

PSALM 56:9

When I cry unto thee, then shall mine enemies turn back:
this I know; for God is for me.

Although it seems to confuse the order of these selections right at the outset, I have chosen to begin my discussion of individual passages with this one because I believe all confidence, all comfort, all strength, all safety starts here—"This I know; . . . God is for me." That truth has to be seared into our hearts, written in bold letters across the tissue of our brains, and never forgotten. Like the blood of the Passover with which ancient Israelites were to mark the lintel and side posts of their doors, we ought to have some such figurative reminder constantly before our eyes and always in our hearts that God is for us. Whenever we go out and always when we come in, no matter what the trouble and trial of the day may be, we start and finish with the eternal truth that God is for us. He loves us. He is our Heavenly Father. He never sleeps nor slumbers in His watchcare over us. His work and His glory are to save us, to exalt us, to see us safely home with Him.

Everything He does is in support of that ultimate purpose, no matter what refinements or trials are required in the achievement of that objective. Acknowledging the dimensions of His majesty and all quantum physics of the universe, from the budding of a flower in spring to expanding realms of galaxies without number, God's singular, solitary quest is to bless and exalt His children, to save (if they will let Him) every human soul.

So in our efforts to swim through our sea of troubles, we must master this thought; in the common parlance of our faith, we must get a testimony of it. *God is for us.* He is *never* against us. We and all others have the freedom, the eternal agency, to make choices, including stupid or cruel or evil ones. Because of this He can be against things we do and against things that others do to us. He will always be against sin, abuse, and error in whatever form they come and from whomever they may flow. But even then He has the divine ability to separate His opposition to the sin from His unyielding love for the sinner. We may not be very good at making that fine distinction, but He is perfect at it and has had a lot of practice.

In, through, and around all of the human, societal, and natural difficulties in our mortal world, God always loves us. *He is always for us.* In His divinity He cannot do or be otherwise. He would have no reason to be if it were otherwise. It is His nature to love His children. There are certain qualities and virtues that are inseparable from godhood. One of them—the principal one—is His unfailing, unfaltering, unflagging love for His children. We are trying to achieve those divine attributes, but He already has them. If He were to betray them or leave them or compromise them, He would "cease to be God."[21] But He is never going to cease being God and He is never going to compromise the virtues and characteristics of His godhood.

So we will find ourselves better prepared to carry on in the face of difficulty, to go forward with true faith, if we can hold to a few rock-solid principles that will undergird us on our way. The very first of those, the most fundamental of all, must be that God lives and does love us—that *He is for us.* And as the Apostle Paul would later ask, "If God be for us, who [or we might add, what] can be against us? . . . We are more than conquerors through him that loved us."[22]

PSALM 1:1–3

Blessed is the man that walketh not in the counsel of the ungodly, nor standeth in the way of sinners, nor sitteth in the seat of the scornful.

But his delight is in the law of the Lord; and in his law doth he meditate day and night.

And he shall be like a tree planted by the rivers of water, that bringeth forth his fruit in his season; his leaf also shall not wither; and whatsoever he doeth shall prosper.

One of the implications of God's existence and fatherly concern for us is that He will tell us things we need to know in order for us to succeed. Indeed, one of the woes we hear in a world that has not embraced the Restoration of the gospel is the lament that God no longer speaks—with the terrible follow-on thought that He must therefore no longer care. Well, He does care, and He has from the beginning. He does speak, and this counsel, including revelation in the present day, becomes for us His law.

His laws—in the scriptures they are appropriately termed "commandments"—are linked to the verities that have come down through eternity. They are the rules for righteous living that have always existed and that He has always taught. As a first step in avoiding heartache and sidestepping as many difficulties as possible, it is incumbent upon us to "delight . . . in the law of the Lord" and think about His commandments always, "meditate day and night" upon them. We cannot do what we have not learned, and we cannot obey what we have not been taught. The teachings of God's prophets, living and dead, which outline and underscore the laws of God, are our rod of iron to which we must hold resolutely as we make our way through the mists of darkness in this life.[23]

Not all trials and tribulations we face come as a result of breaking the commandments, but some of them do. Obviously, there are some problems we probably cannot avoid; although we try to be obedient to the principles of the gospel, still some challenges come. But undoubtedly in each of our lives there are problems we *could* have avoided by greater understanding of God's declarations and more faithfulness in adhering to that counsel. We must see these divine directions as among our greatest gifts and not a burdensome set of restrictions designed to rob us of spontaneity and freedom. No, the laws of the Lord lead to "the way, the truth, and the life."[24] The fact of the matter is, we have the potential in mortality to be lost much of the time. We need to be shown how to come out safely. That is the function of the law of the Lord, the protective counsel of the commandments from those who know the way and He who *is* the Way.

And lest it be overlooked, note the painful observation with which this first psalm begins. It is intended to be something of a backdrop against which all the psalms that follow are considered. It is the reminder that in the quest for a peaceful and productive life, we shouldn't be so foolish as to *choose* trouble. Life is difficult enough without our adding stupidity to our list of mistakes. How frustrating it must be to God when, wanting to help us and knowing full well the dangers along the way, He sees us willingly, willfully choose to walk in the counsel of the ungodly, stand in the way of sinners, and sit in the seat of the scornful. Even when we give the ungodly, the sinner, and the scorner wide berth, there will still be problems for us to face, so how foolish then—frankly "foolish" doesn't seem quite strong enough—to walk *toward* trouble, to stand right in the midst of troublemakers, to sit with those who would rob us of our faith and our efforts to be obedient. We ought, like Joseph in Egypt, to flee, to simply turn and run from such temptation and trouble.[25]

We are asking a lot of God when we consciously break His commandments, then cry unto Him about our troubles and ask His deliverance from that which we could have done more to avoid in the first place. As noted, that is not the case with all of our challenges, but we are rather painfully left without much excuse regarding those challenges we face that we could have avoided by delighting in the law of the Lord and remembering the commandments day and night. Thank heaven—literally—that God will help us even when we are our own worst enemy, but we ought to try harder not to make His job any more difficult than it already is. Meditate on His laws. Strive to keep His commandments. Avoid all the problems you can. Try to be true. Then we can justifiably ask Him to take care of the rest. Then the leaves on our own little tree of life will not wither, and the fruit we so much want to harvest will be bountiful in every season.

PSALM 3:2–5

Many there be which say of my soul, There is no help for him in God.

But thou, O Lord, art a shield for me; my glory, and the lifter up of mine head.

I cried unto the Lord with my voice, and he heard me out of his holy hill. . . .

I laid me down and slept; I awaked; for the Lord sustained me.

Surely in our increasingly secular, post-modern world there are legions who will say to the grief-stricken or disappointed, "There is no help for him in God." But there *is* help in God. He will hear our cries "out of his holy hill." God *always* hears our prayers and He *always* answers them. We may not hear His answers, or we may not recognize His answers if we do hear them, and in some cases we may not like His answers even though we say we trust Him. In those moments especially, we must remember He is a "shield." And one of the things we need to be shielded against is ourselves. We must constantly remind ourselves that He is God and we are not. So when we have a choice between His view of our need and our own, we must yield to His divine view and His divine love.

There are two other reminders in this psalm. The first is that when times are trying, we must keep our heads up. We can't see the rising of the sun or the silver lining on a cloud or God's glory anywhere if we are always looking at the stones in our path. As an angel once said to an ancient prophet who was himself "weighed down with sorrow," "Lift up thy head and rejoice, for thou hast great cause to rejoice."[26] "Lift up your eyes," Jesus once urged His young and inexperienced disciples.[27] Every great cause requires vision. We have to see before we can achieve. God will be "the lifter up of [our] head" if we will give Him a chance to do so.

An even more practical piece of advice in this psalm is to "sleep on it." The Psalmist says, "I laid me down and slept; I awaked; for the Lord sustained me." Not all problems disappear with a night's sleep, but our ability to face them and see more constructive approaches to them improves dramatically with rest. Macbeth speaks for everyone who has trouble when he longs for sleep that "knits up the raveled sleave of care . . . [and is] the balm of hurt minds."[28] There was divine wisdom in putting a night between two days. Don't make important decisions or try to resolve serious problems when you are exhausted. Get some sleep. Your mind will be refreshed and your spirit will be quickened. You will have new strength for the task. God will hear you in His holy hill and with a lifted head you will see a new day dawning. "In returning and rest shall ye be saved; in quietness and in confidence shall be your strength."[29]

PSALM 4:1

Hear me when I call, O God of my righteousness: thou hast enlarged me when I was in distress; have mercy upon me, and hear my prayer.

Quite regularly in life we all have the personal, even painful need for relief from some kind of despair. We all cry out to our Father in Heaven, "Hear my prayer."

If that relief is not as immediately forthcoming as we would like, we must remember that in those times of distress, God "enlarges" us, makes us grow, makes us stretch, requires more of us than we are wanting (or sometimes willing) to require of ourselves. Our purpose in life is to grow in godly ways, to be enlarged in such virtues as faith, hope, and charity, patience, perseverance, and strength. If that growth must come through sorrow or distress or grief, then so be it. It will be all right in the end. One who would learn to run must first learn to walk, and one who would walk must first learn to stand. We are pursuing a divine plan that will one day lift us above all distress, but it will take many prayers—and many answers to them—before we are victorious. With Isaiah I say, take heart:

"Hast though not known? hast thou not heard, that the

everlasting God, the Lord, the Creator of the ends of the earth, fainteth not, neither is weary? . . .

"He giveth power to the faint; and to them that have no might he increaseth strength. . . .

"They that wait upon the Lord shall renew their strength; they shall mount up with wings as eagles; they shall run, and not be weary; and they shall walk, and not faint."[30]

Thus distress enlarges us, eventually lifts us as "with wings [of] eagles." Stay in the race. Keep running. Keep walking. Keep praying. The Lord will renew your strength.

PSALMS 4:4; 27:14; 46:10

Stand in awe, and sin not: commune with your own heart upon your bed, and be still.

Wait on the Lord: be of good courage, and he shall strengthen thine heart: wait, I say, on the Lord.

Be still, and know that I am God: I will be exalted among the heathen, I will be exalted in the earth.

Often in our lives we get so focused on our own circumstances and problems that we fail to "stand in awe" of who God truly is and what He has done in His majesty. Job, the archetype of the righteous sufferer, was guilty of that—as we all are from time to time. Job had asked the Lord so many questions that the Lord felt to ask Job a few. "Who is this that darkeneth counsel by words without knowledge?" God asks. "Where wast thou when I laid the foundations of the earth? . . . Whereupon are the foundations thereof fastened? or who laid the corner stone thereof[?] . . . Or who shut up the sea with doors, when it brake forth . . . and said, Hitherto shalt thou come, but no further . . . ?"[31] And so He goes, asking Job about life and death, darkness and light, snowstorms and rosebuds, the constellations in the heavens.

As the questions continue—questions to which neither Job nor any mortal man has answers—the Lord then asks, "Wilt thou condemn me"?[32] Not, we are told, unless we are God's equal. Not unless we too can do His work. Not unless we have "an arm like God."[33]

Job says in his humility and some embarrassment, "I uttered that I understood not; things too wonderful for me, which I knew not. . . . Wherefore I abhor myself, and repent in dust and ashes."[34]

We don't need to abhor ourselves, but we may need to repent a little when we too are tempted to shake our fists at God and demand, "Why?" or "Why me?" or "Why now?" or "Why this?" We can't know the answer to those questions until we know God—until we have done what He has done and seen what He has seen. None of us have done that yet.

So, in times of trouble, we are to "stand in awe, and sin not." No fewer than a dozen times in scripture the Lord commands His prophets to "stand still." We are to be a little quieter, be a little calmer. We are to "commune with [our] own heart . . . and be still." With such perspective we will both live and sleep in greater peace and safety.

To reinforce this truth God has said—again—to the Saints of our own day, "Stop, and stand still . . . I will provide means whereby thou mayest accomplish this thing which I have commanded thee."[35] He is "exalted in [and above] the earth," and He can similarly lift us above all our trials if we will "cheerfully do all things that lie in our power; and then . . . stand still, with the utmost assurance, to see the salvation of God, and for his arm to be revealed."[36]

One of my brethren, a modern Apostle who has faced overwhelming health challenges—staggering challenges against which a lesser man would simply have given up—said in a general conference of the Church: "Waiting upon the Lord means to 'stand fast' . . . [and to say] 'Thy will be done, O Lord, and not ours.' As we wait upon the Lord, we are 'immovable in keeping the commandments.'" He then concluded with the promise of Isaiah cited earlier—to run and not be weary, and to walk and not faint.[37] For one who may never again run or walk unaided in this life, that is true courage. He is one who is willing to stand still and wait upon the Lord.

If God can from time to time tell His prophets to wait, He surely can and will tell us the same thing. On those occasions, the most courageous stand we can take is just that—to stand, to be patient, to be still, to believe that there will be victory even if the victory is not to come now. Be of good courage. The Lord will strengthen thy heart.

PSALM 4:6–7

There be many that say, Who will shew us any good? Lord, lift thou up the light of thy countenance upon us.

Thou hast put gladness in my heart, more than in the time that their corn and their wine increased.

In times of trouble or despair we often find ourselves feeling that, because something has gone wrong, everything has gone wrong. As the Psalmist notes, we say, "Who will show us *any* good?" as if to assert that in times of sorrow or want there isn't *anything* good in life or in nature or in all of humankind. In answer to that lament, the Psalmist calls for the light of God's countenance to smile upon His children, to roll back the darkness and lift the shadows from the scene.

There is so much that is good all around us, so much to make us glad even beyond the traditional joy of the harvest season, when the bounties of the field and the vineyard remind us now as well as anciently just how good God is to us.

Those who say there is no love in the world have never seen a mother gaze into the eyes of her newborn child. Those who say there is no beauty in the world have never seen New England in the fall or old England in the spring or the Swiss lakes and landscapes any time of the year. Those who say there is no harmony in the world have never heard Brahms or Beethoven, Puccini or Vivaldi. Who hasn't had a sudden intake of breath when first seeing the art of Michelangelo or Titian, Rembrandt or Matisse, Constable or Monet? And what of all the widespread blessings of science, medicine, communication, and transportation? Wherever we look, there are wonders of things in heaven and on earth.

"Who will shew us any good?" A child will, a neighbor will, a friend will, and so will our Father in Heaven. "Lord, lift thou up the light of thy countenance upon us. Thou hast put gladness in my heart, more than in the time that their corn and their wine increased."

PSALMS 5:1; 119:15, 48

Give ear to my words, O Lord, consider my meditation.

I will meditate in thy precepts, and have respect unto thy ways. . . .

My hands also will I lift up unto thy commandments, which I have loved; and I will meditate in thy statutes.

An earlier psalm counseled us to "commune with your own heart."[38] This psalm gives that practice a name—meditation. None of us are alone with our own thoughts, prayers, dreams, and reflections as much as we ought to be. "The world is too much with us," Wordsworth said,[39] and that world is often noisy, brash, raucous, and vulgar. It would seem that most of what the everyday world offers is calculated *not* to let us meditate, *not* to let us commune with our own heart.

Deadlines, car pools, telephones, and to-do lists. Horns honking, bells ringing, numbers to memorize, and people to meet. We need some peace and quiet. We need some quiet and peace. And our circumstances are often such that we cannot "get away" to the summit of a mountain or a quiet stretch of seashore. Sometimes we can't even get to the city park. But we should try to "get away" into our inner space, into that quiet spiritual center God gave every one of us. Nowhere can anyone find a quieter or more untroubled retreat than in his or her own soul. We need to turn some things down and turn some things off. We need to be quiet.

President David O. McKay taught: "We pay too little attention to the value of meditation, a principle of devotion. In our worship there are two elements: One is spiritual communion arising from our own meditation; the other, instruction from others, particularly from those who have authority to guide and instruct us. Of the two, the more profitable introspectively is the meditation. Meditation is the language of the soul. It is defined as 'a form of private devotion, or spiritual exercise, consisting in deep, continued reflection on some religious theme.' Meditation is a form of prayer."[40]

Part of the reason I find meditation so precious is that it allows God to speak to me. Prayer, for the most part, is our urgent speaking to Him. We have a lot on our minds. We have a lot in our hearts. We have many needs and wants and wishes. My prayers are sometimes filled almost completely with a laundry list of requests.

In such urgent need there is a temptation not to listen before and during and after our spoken prayers. Too seldom do we prepare to pray, and too seldom do we quietly reflect after our prayers. These are times for reverent meditation. They allow our minds and our hearts to communicate clearly—and to be communicated to clearly—without words, or at least without spoken words.

Spoken words are crucial. Vocal prayer is a fundamental requirement in gospel living. The Savior has asked us all to pray as He prayed. But surely we should also meditate as He meditated, thinking of God quietly, reverently, and often. In our religious discourse we speak of the whisperings of the Spirit. We need to listen for those whisperings. They are still and they are small—but they are essential. Meditation is one of the methods by which we show "respect unto [God's] ways."

PSALM 5:11–12

But let all those that put their trust in thee rejoice: let them ever shout for joy, because thou defendest them: let them also that love thy name be joyful in thee.

For thou, Lord, wilt bless the righteous; with favour wilt thou compass him as with a shield.

"Men are, that they might have joy," Lehi declared to Jacob,[41] but some days, joy seems to be in short supply. However, the Psalmist gives us the truest counsel that can be given for obtaining and keeping that elusive delight. We are to put our trust in the Lord and shout for joy that He is our defender, our protector, our benefactor, our God. Just to hear His name triggers thoughts of His character and goodness. Names do that when we think of people we love. The sacred name of God—which we are commanded not to take in vain—is a source of joy unequaled, bringing to us a sense of being dearly loved and completely safe, encompassed "as with a shield."

St. Augustine once observed that men wish to be happy even when they live so as to make happiness impossible. What a blessing, then—or at least it ought to be—when a key is given as to how we can make happiness possible. How often people come toward joy like a child to a shop window, gazing inside with great sadness that they do not have the coins to make a purchase, when in fact the item we long for is free. It is every shopper's gift just for the taking. "He that hath no money; come ye, buy, and eat; yea, come, buy wine and milk without money and without price."[42] True joy is available for the same price. Put your trust in God. Love Him and love His name. Hearken diligently unto Him.

"True joy is the earnest [money] which we have of heaven," wrote one of England's greatest cleric/poets. "It is the treasure of the soul, and therefore should be laid in a safe place, and nothing in this world is safe to place it in."[43] If we want real joy, we must put our trust in God. The return on that investment will be joy and shielded protection—with an eternal increase in the process.

PSALMS 6:2–4, 6, 8; 57:1

Have mercy upon me, O Lord; for I am weak: O Lord, heal me; for my bones are vexed.

My soul is also sore vexed: but thou, O Lord, how long?

Return, O Lord, deliver my soul: oh save me for thy mercies' sake. . . .

I am weary with my groaning; all the night make I my bed to swim; I water my couch with my tears. . . .

Depart from me, all ye workers of iniquity; for the Lord hath heard the voice of my weeping.

Be merciful unto me, O God, be merciful unto me: for my soul trusteth in thee: yea, in the shadow of thy wings will I make my refuge, until these calamaties be overpast.

Every one of us has occasion—often frequent occasion—to cry out that not only our bones but also our souls are "vexed." And sometimes that vexing goes on and on. At such times we have occasion also to cry out, "O Lord, how long?" as did the Prophet Joseph Smith in Liberty Jail.[44] As the Psalmist says later in this collection, "How long wilt thou forget me, O Lord? for ever? how long wilt thou hide thy face from me?"[45] So, too, did the Prophet Joseph cry out in his feelings of abandonment, "O God, where art thou? And where is the pavilion that covereth thy hiding place? How long shall thy hand be stayed, and thine eye, . . . yea, O Lord, how long shall . . . these wrongs and unlawful oppressions" continue?[46]

Sometimes these woes come just because life has its troubles, but other times they come from actual "workers of iniquity." Such was the case with the Prophet Joseph Smith's trials, and such might be the case with ours as well. Nevertheless, we need to remember that even in such extremities, even when we have suffered "wrongs and unlawful oppressions," God is still with us and still whispers, "peace be unto thy soul."[47]

In encouraging us to be peaceful in such difficult times, He asks us to remember these things:

First, our adversity and affliction shall be but a small moment. Our trials seem to be long-lasting—or everlasting—when we are in the midst of them, but they do come to an end. With an eternal view, they really are of a small moment. When we have done all we know how to do to prevent a problem or redress a wrong, sometimes all we can do is endure. Often enough in our mortal struggle the only response we can make is to hang on and hide in "the shadow of [God's] wings . . . until these calamities be overpast." Difficulties do pass, hard times end, the trouble we thought would never go away goes away. So there is hope, not simple stoicism, in enduring.

Second, if we endure our challenges well, God will exalt us on high and we will triumph over our foes, whether those foes be actual people seeking to do us harm or simply the vicissitudes of life that bring grief and trouble with them. In any case, we are promised that we will rise above and conquer our foes.

Third, we need to remember that we do have friends. Thank heaven for friends! The Prophet Joseph was reminded that his friends were still standing by him and that they would yet hail him again with "warm hearts and friendly hands."[48]

Fourth, in our despair, there can always be a tendency to self-pity. We need to resist that at all costs, for it damages everything it touches. We need to remember that we are "not yet as Job."[49] We have many, many blessings, and there are many, many people in the world who face far more difficult circumstances than do we.

All of this can help dry our tears, but that is not to say tears don't come. The Psalmist has wept so much his bed is "swimming." Near the end of his life, the prophet Nephi said he "water[ed his] pillow by night" praying for his people.[50] The "voice of . . . weeping" is part of mortal experience. Tears are all right. They are the price we pay for love, care, and compassion in the world. One day God will, in great victory, "wipe away all tears from their eyes; and there shall be no more death, neither sorrow, nor crying, neither shall there be any more pain: for the former things are passed away."[51] One day our calamities will be overpast.

PSALM 8:2

Out of the mouth of babes and sucklings hast thou ordained strength because of thine enemies, that thou mightest still the enemy and the avenger.

One of the most moving accounts ever recorded in the Book of Mormon (may I say ever recorded in *any* scripture?) is the account of Christ appearing to the Nephites and, after a full day of teaching and testifying, gathering the children at His feet. Then, praying profoundly for these little ones, "he wept, . . . and . . . took their little children, one by one, and blessed them, and prayed unto the Father for them. And when he had done this he wept again; and he spake unto the multitude, and said unto them: Behold your little ones."[52] Then the heavens opened and angels descended and ministered unto them, encircling the little children as if with fire.

But this is not all. In the days that followed, Jesus "did teach and minister unto the children of the multitude of whom hath been spoken, and . . . even babes did open their mouths and utter marvelous things; and the things which they did utter were forbidden that there should not any man write them."[53]

Given the power and majesty of the teachings the Savior had

given these Nephites—including the calling of the Twelve Nephite disciples, the sermon at the temple, prophecies about the tribes of Israel, clarification regarding the law of Moses, introduction of the sacramental ordinance, great discourses on prayer and the Holy Ghost, to name just a few—it is amazing to think that what these children knew and said was even greater than the things Jesus taught their parents. Nevertheless, the book says of the children, "He did loose their tongues, and they did speak unto their fathers great and marvelous things, even greater than he [Jesus] had revealed unto the people."[54]

The prophet Alma taught: "[God] imparteth his word by angels unto men, yea, not only men but women also. Now this is not all; little children do have words given unto them many times, which confound the wise and the learned."[55]

We all cherish our children. Mine mean more to me—and to their mother—than any possession we own. All of us can respect our children and listen to them. In so many ways we need to be more like them, because "of such is the kingdom of heaven."[56] Children come "trailing clouds of glory . . . from God, who is [their] home,"[57] and thereby they will frequently be the source of God's inspiration and utterance to us. Even in the most trying of times, we cannot remain despondent when holding a baby or looking into the innocent, wonder-filled eyes of a child. As their bodies grow, so does their enthusiasm—brimming, bubbling, and contagious with energy too great to be contained in little bodies. No trouble can overwhelm the delight of childhood. "Out of the mouth of babes and sucklings [God has] ordained strength."

PSALM 11:1

*In the Lord put I my trust: how say ye to my soul, Flee as a
bird to your mountain?*

Sometimes when life is complex and demanding we simply need
to "get away." This is not to be confused with "run away," but it
is to go—physically, if possible, but in any case spiritually, mentally,
and emotionally—to a mountain or some other favorite place of renewal. Sometimes we need to fly like a bird, and in so doing find the
freedom to regroup and renew. Then we can return to the fray with
stronger faith and greater hope, renewed vigor for the battle of life.

Jesus did this as often as possible. When the crowds were too
great on the seashore, He would put out in a boat and cross to the
other side of the lake. When the bustle—and often hostility—of
Jerusalem was too great, He would retreat to His beloved Galilee.
When the throngs in the street or the marketplace were too great, He
would "flee as a bird" to His mountain.

*And when he had sent the multitudes away, he went up into
a mountain apart to pray: and when the evening was come, he
was there alone.*[58]

And again:

When it was day, he departed and went into a desert place: and the people sought him, and came unto him, and stayed him, that he should not depart from them.[59]

And again:

And in the morning, rising up a great while before day, he went out, and departed into a solitary place, and there prayed,
And Simon and they that were with him followed after him.
And when they had found him, they said unto him, All men seek for thee.[60]

And again:

They were filled with madness; and communed one with another what they might do to Jesus.
And it came to pass in those days, that he went out into a mountain to pray, and continued all night in prayer to God.[61]

Life is demanding. Our days are complex. People's needs are great. We are expected to fight the good fight. That is our purpose and duty. But to do so we need renewal physically, we need refreshment spiritually, and we need peace emotionally. To do so we need time with God and ourselves. We need solitude. We need the strength that fleeing as a bird to our holy mountain will provide.

PSALMS 15:1–3; 17:3; 34:13

Lord, who shall abide in thy tabernacle? who shall dwell in thy holy hill?

He that walketh uprightly, and worketh righteousness, and speaketh the truth in his heart.

He that backbiteth not with his tongue, nor doeth evil to his neighbour, nor taketh up a reproach against his neighbour.

Thou hast proved mine heart; thou hast visited me in the night; thou hast tried me, and shalt find nothing; I am purposed that my mouth shall not transgress.

Keep thy tongue from evil, and thy lips from speaking guile.

The early Brethren in our dispensation deepened our understanding of the power of speech when they taught, "*It is by words . . . [that] every being works when he works by faith. God said, 'Let there be light: and there was light.' Joshua spake, and the great* lights which God had created stood still. Elijah commanded, and the heavens were stayed for the space of three years and six months, so that it did not rain. . . . All this was done by faith. . . . *Faith, then, works by words; and with [words] its mightiest works have been, and will be, performed.*"[62] Like all gifts "which cometh from above," words are "sacred, and must be spoken with care, and by constraint of the Spirit."[63] Words are so powerful that sometimes we need to assess how we speak to each other and even how we speak of ourselves.

There is a line from the Apocrypha that puts the seriousness of this issue better than I can. It reads, "The stroke of the whip maketh marks in the flesh: but the stroke of the tongue breaketh the bones."[64] With that stinging image in mind, it is worth noting what James, the brother of Jesus, said about "a perfect man": "For in many things we offend all. *[But] if any man offend not in word, the same is a perfect man,* and able also to bridle the whole body."

Continuing the imagery of the bridle, James writes: "Behold, we put bits in the horses' mouths, that they may obey us; and we turn about their whole body.

"Behold also . . . ships, which though they be . . . great, and are driven of fierce winds, yet are they turned about with a very small helm."

Then he makes his point: "The tongue is [also] a little member. . . . [But] behold, how great a [forest][65] a little fire [can burn].

" . . . So is the tongue [a fire] among our members, . . . it defileth the whole body, . . . it is set on fire of hell.

"For every kind of beasts, and of birds, and of serpents, and of things in the sea, . . . hath been tamed of mankind:

"But the tongue can no man tame; it is an unruly evil, full of deadly poison.

"Therewith bless we God, even the Father; and therewith curse we men, which are made after the similitude of God.

"Out of the same mouth proceedeth blessing and cursing. My brethren, these things ought not so to be."[66]

That is pretty straightforward, to say the least. Obviously James doesn't mean our tongues are always iniquitous, nor that everything we say is "full of deadly poison." But he clearly means that at least some things we say can be destructive, even venomous—and that is a chilling indictment! The voice that bears profound testimony, utters fervent prayer, and sings lovely hymns *can be* the same voice that berates and criticizes, embarrasses and demeans, inflicts pain and destroys the spirit of oneself and of others in the process. "Out of the same mouth proceedeth blessing and cursing," James grieves. "My brethren [and sisters], these things ought not so to be."

Paul put it candidly, but very hopefully. He said to all of us: "Let no corrupt communication proceed out of your mouth, but [only] that which is good . . . [and] edifying, that it may minister grace unto the hearers.

"And grieve not the holy Spirit of God. . . .

"Let all bitterness, and wrath, and anger, and clamour, and evil speaking, be put away from you. . . .

"And be ye kind one to another, tenderhearted, forgiving one another, even as God for Christ's sake hath forgiven you."[67]

We should all try for at least *this* form of perfection—that we bridle our tongues when they need to be bridled, that we will not transgress with our mouth.

PSALM 17:8

Keep me as the apple of the eye, hide me under the shadow of thy wings.

A world-renowned authority on child development once said that every child deserves to have someone in his or her life who is absolutely crazy about them. Unfortunately, in mortal living and temporal existence, that is not always the good fortune of every child. But it is true that, in a wonderful way known only to Him, God can see every child, every individual born on the earth, as "the apple of [His] eye." We do not know how that divine compassion can be so broad and still be so individualistic, but it is. Somehow God can focus on every one of us personally, know the concerns and fears of each one of us uniquely. In those times of our need, it is as if no other voice distracts Him, no other need in the universe diverts Him. In those moments when we especially need Him, in times of trouble or otherwise, we are seemingly the sole object of His affection and attention. We are the "apple of [His] eye" and, like the protective, vigilant parent that He is, He hides us "under the shadow of [His] wings." Every child—of whatever age—can take great comfort from that, especially in times of trouble.

PSALM 17:8

Keep me as the apple of the eye, hide me under the shadow of thy wings.

PSALMS 18:2, 30; 61:2; 62:6

The Lord is my rock, and my fortress, and my deliverer; my God, my strength, in whom I will trust; my buckler, and the horn of my salvation, and my high tower. . . .

As for God, his way is perfect: the word of the Lord is tried: he is a buckler to all those that trust in him.

———————

From the end of the earth will I cry unto thee, when my heart is overwhelmed: lead me to the rock that is higher than I.

———————

He only is my rock and my salvation: he is my defence; I shall not be moved.

Among the most reassuring images in the psalms and other scriptures is the portrayal of God as a rock or a fortress. He is rock solid, rock strong, rock sure. He is firm. He can't be overwhelmed or overcome. But life is such that the rest of us don't always feel so solid, so strong, or so sure. Circumstances often knock us off balance, and we stagger a bit. We face events that are disorienting to us, that make us uneasy or uncertain or downright fearful.

How wonderful it is in such times to have a rock to lean on, or a high tower to flee to. How wonderful it is when our foot is slipping or our faith is sliding to know that there is something firm and immovable—something solid—that can shore us up and stabilize our uneasiness.

The Book of Mormon prophet Helaman said to his sons Nephi and Lehi, "Remember that it is upon the rock of our Redeemer, who is Christ, the Son of God, that ye must build your foundation; that when the devil shall send forth his mighty winds, yea, his shafts in the whirlwind, yea, when all his hail and his mighty storm shall beat upon you, it shall have no power over you to drag you down to the gulf of misery and endless wo, because of the rock upon which ye are built, which is a sure foundation, a foundation whereon if men build they cannot fall."[68]

And, of course, what we say of the Son we say of the Father. As beloved Hannah prayed, so pray we, "There is none holy as the Lord: for there is none beside thee: neither is there any rock like our God."[69]

With the Father and the Son, the Holy Ghost and the gospel as anchors to our lives, we stand more fit and fortified to face life's challenges. These are our deliverers. These are as unmoved and unmovable as they are unfailing. We trust them, and therein is our salvation.

"Therefore, fear not, little flock; do good; let earth and hell combine against you, for if ye are built upon my rock, they cannot prevail."[70]

PSALMS 18:36; 94:18–19

Thou hast enlarged my steps under me, that my feet did not slip.

When I said, My foot slippeth; thy mercy, O Lord, held me up.

In the multitude of my thoughts within me thy comforts delight my soul.

When we allow God to come into our lives (or we are wise enough to come into His) He "enlarges our steps" for the path we must walk—or, in more modern language, He gives us bigger feet that do not slip.

Much of the miraculous help we find in the gospel is just that—a miracle from heaven, the power of divine priesthood, the attendance of angels administering to us through a very thin veil. These are gifts from God, manifestations of His grace. They are provided for us without much control or power—or even much worthiness, it seems—on our part.

But other elements of God's miraculous help consist of things

He does to, in effect, let us help ourselves. Some paths we feel we just can't walk. Some mountains seem just too high to climb. Some steps are just too difficult to take. When that is so, heaven does intervene, but often it is not to smooth out the path or remove the mountain or shorten the steps. More often than not, God sends help in a different way. He makes us stronger and more sure-footed. In effect, He gives us bigger feet, stronger legs, a firmer back, more stiffened shoulders. He deals with us rather than with the problem we face. We then proceed with new strength, less slipping, and are all the stronger for it.

A case in point is recorded in Book of Mormon history. In a very difficult circumstance, "the burdens which were laid upon Alma and his brethren were made light; yea, the Lord did strengthen them that they could bear up their burdens with ease."[71] The trials were still there, but the backs of the people were made equal to the burdens the Lord placed upon them.

Time and again, over and over, more than we give Him credit for, the Lord steadies us in those moments when we slip. He secures our footing. He keeps us from falling. Obviously, some people we know have not only slipped but taken a brutal nosedive. However, even in those mistakes He can pick us up, dress our wounds, and put us on our way again.

But we would do well to pause and give consideration to the dozens of times, the hundreds of times that we *didn't* slip. Perhaps through our own ignorance or insistence, we should have. But we didn't. His mercy held us up. Life holds many recognizable near misses, but there are many, many more that are *not* recognized, the consequences of which we never knew, the danger of which never came to be. Before our foot slipped—or even as it started to slip—we were taken to safety. In the multitude of those thoughts, those memories and chances when something might have happened differently and tragically (but didn't!), "thy comforts delight my soul."

PSALMS 19:1–3; 8:3–6

The heavens declare the glory of God; and the firmament sheweth his handywork.

Day unto day uttereth speech, and night unto night sheweth knowledge.

There is no speech nor language, where their voice is not heard.

When I consider thy heavens, the work of thy fingers, the moon and the stars, which thou hast ordained;

What is man, that thou art mindful of him? and the son of man, that thou visitest him?

For thou hast made him a little lower than the angels, and hast crowned him with glory and honour.

Thou madest him to have dominion over the works of thy hands; thou hast put all things under his feet.

When the antichrist Korihor defiantly and arrogantly asked Alma for a sign of God's presence and power, Alma said peremptorily, "Thou hast had signs enough." And the greatest of those signs was the everlasting evidence of "the earth, and all things that are upon the face of it, yea, and its motion, yea, and also all the planets which move in their regular form." For as far as either the ancient or modern eye can see, these "do witness that there is a Supreme Creator."[72]

Among the most humbling and thrilling experiences available to us in mortality are the occasional glimpses we have into immortality when we view the wonder of God's creations. These wonders could be the colorful splendor of a beautiful autumn or the reawakening that comes so dramatically in spring. They could be majestic mountains or glacial fjords. The beauty of such divine handiwork comes in hundreds of varieties on the earth and (somehow even more awesome to the eye) in a dark night's gaze into the heavens.

For me personally, no view in mortality is more awe-inspiring than standing alone on a night completely void of earthly light and seeing the star-filled heavens fully appear. To me it is the most overwhelming view in nature. Of course, what we see with the naked eye is only a small part of one—our own—tiny little galaxy. Aided by the magnificent lenses of space telescopes and galactic photography, we can see more of other "worlds without number."[73] Truly "night [after] night sheweth knowledge," the knowledge of God. And there is no country or culture on this entire planet over which the stars are not constantly shining, constantly testifying of His omniscience and omnipotence. Neither is there any limit to space, any spot in the universe where the majesty of God's creation is not unfolding. All these things are "the work of [God's] fingers."

And yet the greatest of all His works is a man, a woman, a child, any "ordinary" being who walks among us. Some of those people are in trouble, some have had great misfortune, some have had difficulties through no fault of their own, and some have had burdens that were in great measure of their own making. But whatever condition they may be in, the greatest of God's creations are His children—us. In all of those heavenly creations that are so stunning to see on a clear, starry night, we are the ones that are just "a little lower than the angels," which in Hebrew is rendered "a little lower than Elohim [the Gods]." As such, we are crowned with glory and honor here and with the promise of glory and honor there.

C. S. Lewis once said that if we could recognize who we were, we would realize that we were walking with "possible gods and goddesses" whom, if we could see them in all their eternal dignity and glory, we would be tempted to fall down and worship.[74] Because this is true, we need to think more highly of ourselves and we need to think more highly of each other. In all of God's creations, mortal men and women are His greatest work and the only portion of His creation to carry the actual life-giving seeds of His eternal splendor, the chance to perpetuate the glory of such great creations. We need to think more about that when a baby is born, and we need to think more about that when some of those babies grow up to face trouble. We need to continue thinking highly of them and to be helpful to them. We need to honor the divinity that is within all humankind. In doing so, we will be returning to God at least some of that glory and honor with which He has crowned us.

In a world—or should we say, in a universe—of large troubles and small, a world of physical, financial, political, and social forces seemingly beyond our control, there can be moments when we also wonder, "Do I matter in all of this? Can my small and sometimes painful place in the great scheme of things amount to much? Can God know me or have time for me or hear my prayers? With all that needs divine attention in the world—famines, wars, pestilence, sin— can my heart be known, understood, and seen as important in the grand expanse of the universe?" On difficult, discouraging days almost everyone asks such questions.

But the eternal truth, the timeless declaration is "yes" to all of the questions above and more. The great eternal truth is that this entire plan of life, the plan for our salvation, is an outline for each man and woman, each boy and girl, individually. By name, place, and personal circumstance God knows us and our needs. He knows our hopes and dreams and He knows our fears and frustrations. Above all, He knows who we *really* are and what we can become through faith in Him.

Everything that went into those first five days of creation—the rhythm of the universe, the ordering of the planets, the great works of nature, the creation of flora and fauna—all of these are for the sole and solitary purpose of blessing us as individual, eternally valued children of God. One at a time. Each and every one. All of us.

What is man or woman? Who are we really? Even now, in mortality, in our very imperfect state, we are just a little lower than the Gods. As our Heavenly Father's children, we have the inherent capacity to become like Him, to reach our divine potential and achieve our divine destiny. If we will be faithful—literally "full of faith"—*especially* in times of trouble, then we can hear that truth whispered to us as we gaze into the star-filled night.

I wander through the still of night,
When solitude is ev'rywhere—
Alone, beneath the starry light,
And yet I know that God is there.
I kneel upon the grass and pray;
An answer comes without a voice.
It takes my burden all away
And makes my aching heart rejoice.[75]

PSALM 19:13

*Keep back thy servant also from presumptuous sins; let them
not have dominion over me: then shall I be upright, and I shall
be innocent from the great transgression.*

The inevitable question this verse begs is: What are "presumptuous sins"? And why are they at the heart of "the great
transgression"?

The word *presume* comes into the English language from a Latin
root meaning "anticipate" or "assume." In short, a "presumptuous
sin" would be an anticipated one, or, more simply, one that has been
planned.

Transgression is transgression, and all sins are consequential. But
sins we have thought about and planned for, those we have calculated
and anticipated, are "the great transgression." It is one thing to sin
in ignorance or innocence, falling victim to the temptation of the
moment or an uncharacteristic lapse of moral judgment. But surely
it is quite another thing to sin by premeditated planning and design.

On occasion I have heard young people say something like, "I
will sow my wild oats in my youth and then, after I have experienced
the carefree life, I will repent and return to God. There is plenty of

time to do both, and in the end it will be well with me. Besides, I know others who have been sinners in their youth, and they have died firmly in the faith." No statement has terrified me quite like that one. This is "presumptuous sin," and it will be counted by God as "the great transgression." The consequences of this kind of sin will *not* be well with the guilty.

There is peril in playing the prodigal son knowingly, expecting God to forgive us, expecting Christ to bleed for us, expecting mercy to cover us. Among the most grievous sins a mortal can commit is to crucify Christ "afresh,"[76] to knowingly ask Him to suffer on the cross a little longer—or again and again and again—while such an one commits knowingly, with planning and premeditation, his or her "presumptuous sins."

May God protect us from ever presuming on His grace, from presuming on His mercy, from presuming on His forgiveness. May God protect us from all sins, but especially from those we knowingly plan to commit. They are "the great transgression[s]."

PSALM 20:7

Some trust in chariots, and some in horses: but we will re-member the name of the Lord our God.

It is important to remember that the first principle of the gospel is *not* faith in an abstract sense, but specifically "faith in the Lord Jesus Christ."[77] The reason that language is important is because without faith in Christ, faith in anything else is only partial faith or inadequate faith or perhaps even destructive faith. The Psalmist says here that some put their faith in chariots and horses. He might have added flocks and vineyards. He might have added stocks and bonds, houses and careers. He might have added cold cash, personal property, and political influence.

In our day the list of things in which we can put our trust is even more lengthy than that of ancient days because we are so blessed with the riches and luxuries of the earth. We have plenty of newer horses and chariots to tempt us in the twenty-first century. But eventually—as in earlier times—the wheels will grow rusty and the legs will grow lame.

The true purpose of life during the living of it (and at the end of it) is to have put our faith in the things that will not only enrich it but will ultimately outlast it. We should invest in the things that can be taken past the grave into eternal life. And not a single chariot or horse—ancient or modern—is going to make that journey with us.

"Lay not up for yourselves treasures upon earth, where moth and rust doth corrupt, . . . but lay up for yourselves treasures in heaven, . . . for where your treasure is, there will your heart be also."[78]

It is not enough to have faith. We have to have faith in things that save and redeem. And there is only one name given under heaven that can do that. "Remember the name of the Lord our God."

PSALM 22:4–5

Our fathers trusted in thee: they trusted, and thou didst deliver them.

They cried unto thee, and were delivered: they trusted in thee, and were not confounded.

When our problems seem great and the future uncertain, when we wonder whether there is a way out or a way around or a way through, we would do well to remember that our personal (or collective) forebears had the same fears we have and were blessed with help from on high. It gives us hope to remember that others before us needed deliverance and they received it. Sometimes those solutions came quickly, sometimes they came only after months and years, but they came nevertheless.

When the young Nephi needed to rally his brothers to faithful action, he asked them to remember the even more difficult tasks that their fathers had faced in earlier times. "Let us be strong like unto Moses," he said, "for he truly spake unto the waters of the Red Sea and they divided hither and thither, and our fathers came through, out of captivity, on dry ground."[79] We will do better in our hour of

need if we can remember that those before us faced even more challenging troubles than we and still "came through."

A missionary who feels homesick or discouraged needs to remember that those who served before him or her also felt homesick and
discouraged but "came through." A young mother feeling unbear-
able pain over the behavior of a child needs to remember that her
mother before her may have felt the same fear but eventually "was
delivered." Those who face financial loss or professional ruin can take
courage that others have experienced the same thing but they "trusted
in [God]" and worked their way through—probably not easily and
perhaps not soon, but successfully nevertheless.

When difficult times come, remember that others have faced all
of this and more, not the least of whom were our great pioneer fathers and mothers in the early decades of this Church's history. They
walked with faith in every footstep and sought a place "which God
for [them] prepared."[80] They cried unto God and were delivered when
the very thought, the very hope of deliverance, seemed to be furthest
from realization.

We can trust Him to deliver us, too.

PSALMS 24:3–4; 51:10

Who shall ascend into the hill of the Lord? or who shall stand in his holy place?

He that hath clean hands, and a pure heart; who hath not lifted up his soul unto vanity, nor sworn deceitfully.

———————

Create in me a clean heart, O God; and renew a right spirit within me.

Psalm 24, as noted in the introductory chapter of this book, is one of the most quoted—and sung—psalms in all the canon of scripture. A. W. "Mickey" Hart put these words to music. That song has thrilled millions. It still thrills me today whenever I hear it.

The requirements for ascending "into the hill of the Lord" and standing "in his holy place"—as noted earlier, this is a direct reference to the temple—must be many, but here the Psalmist sweetly reduces those requirements to two: purity and humility.

We sometimes hear that the Old Testament and the New Testament are at odds with each other, that they seem to have been written for different purposes to different people. They weren't. In a serious oversimplification, it could be said that much of the Old Testament was dealing with the outer man and the New Testament with the inner, but both are important and both must be addressed in our salvation. To come unto God we must be clean both externally (in our hands) and internally (in our hearts).

Consider the blessing of a baby, or partaking of the sacrament, or participating in temple ordinances. To the degree that we can achieve it, we should literally have clean hands (and clean clothes and clean countenances) for these sacred experiences. We ought to be as clean in appearance as we can be when we seek to stand in God's holy presence. Again in an oversimplification, that might be considered something of an "Old Testament" requirement, but it is a requirement nonetheless.

But in addition to that outward evidence, we must be clean inside as well—pure, if you will—showing the inner state that gives meaning to the outer gesture. We must be clean in thought, innocent in motive, pure in our practices, with no vanity or deceit in us. We must be humble disciples of Christ. This might be considered the "New Testament" requirement of our worthiness to stand in God's presence.

Indeed, purity inside and out may well be the first thing we recognize about the Savior when He returns to rule and reign on earth. As Mormon wrote to his son and the Nephite congregation of that day, "pray unto the Father with all the energy of heart, . . . that ye may become the sons [and daughters] of God; that when he shall appear we shall be like him . . . that we may be purified even as he is pure."[81]

James, the brother of Jesus, shared a lesson for life with us. He said, "The wisdom that is from above is first pure, then peaceable."[82] What a precise, poetic description of the temple and the worthy temple attender. In our day—and with this great dispensation of temple building as a backdrop—we can more fully understand God's determination to "reserve unto myself a pure people." In the house of the Lord we can "be sanctified by that which ye . . . received, and [then] ye shall bind yourselves to act in all holiness before [Him]."[83]

In times of trouble, we can go to the temple, and we must go with clean hands and a pure heart. We will find a "right spirit" renewed within us.

PSALM 25:7

Remember not the sins of my youth, nor my transgressions:
according to thy mercy remember thou me for thy goodness' sake,
O Lord.

No one is as wise in youth as he or she eventually becomes with maturity and age. This is no excuse for transgression, but heaven and the leaders of the Church strive to be generous and forgiving of youthful sins and transgressions. Surely God and the prophets have done everything possible down through time to warn, to caution, to counsel—and, when necessary, to discipline—youth, but at the same time every effort has also been made to help and heal, to assist the young man or young woman to repent and move on, leaving their mistakes behind and realizing what a vast world of opportunity and peace awaits the repentant in their mature years.

Every youth faces "fool's hill" less experienced and less wise than a seasoned person would, but with help—and, if needed, forgiveness—he or she can successfully make it over that hump and on the other side see a life filled with promised blessings and happiness. Every young person who has sinned needs to know that God forgives, that He is a God of mercy, that repentance gives every person—young or old—the chance to overcome errors through the Atonement of the Lord Jesus Christ. Such a gift shouldn't be taken for granted, but fortunately for all of us, this is the gospel of the second chance and the church of the happy ending.

Every youth who is willing to feel sorrow for sin, who will pay the price to seek the Lord's forgiveness and His enabling power to change his or her life, and who will strive to live in a better way no matter what the mistakes of the past have been, is entitled to cry unto the Lord—and be reassured that the plea will be honored—"Remember not the sins of my youth."

One last observation: If God is willing to forgive *and* forget sins truly repented of—"the same is forgiven and I, the Lord, remember them no more"[84]—then surely we must do the same. Nothing is more un-Christian than to keep bringing up past sins—those of others or our own—thereby refusing to let them die. This is to deny the Atonement of Christ. This is to block divine forgiveness. This is to keep alive what God Himself wants buried. Whether it be in a youth or an adult, forgive their transgression. Let the Atonement have full sway. Let the future be bright even if the past wasn't. You and I and all mankind are one day going to plead for such grace. Let's show our Christian discipleship by granting it to others.

PSALM 27:4–5

One thing have I desired of the Lord, that will I seek after;
that I may dwell in the house of the Lord all the days of my life,
to behold the beauty of the Lord, and to enquire in his temple.

For in the time of trouble he shall hide me in his pavilion:
in the secret of his tabernacle shall he hide me; he shall set me up
upon a rock.

For Latter-day Saints, the holiest site on earth is the temple of God, the house of the Lord. It is by definition and dedication a holy place, the setting for God's presence, the earthly structure that allows us heavenly experience. Truly it has been said that all roads in the restored gospel of Jesus Christ lead to the temple, and the temple leads us into eternity. It truly is, in every describable way, a stunningly beautiful place where we can "behold the beauty of the Lord." It is not insignificant that the two greatest—two of the otherwise very, very few—acts of anger recorded about Jesus were in response to the desecration of the temple, His "Father's house,"[85] the place where God descends to man and man ascends to God.

The temple is especially a blessing to us "in the time of trouble."

When a difficult moment comes or an important decision faces us, we instinctively go to the temple. We find peace there and we find answers. It is the setting for tranquillity, purity, and revelation. The tangled complexities of life fall away and the path we should walk or the action we should take—or just the safety and peace we desperately seek—becomes clear. The temple truly is a rock upon which God sets us when the winds and the waves are strongest.

As a practical matter we cannot be in the temple always, and we don't really go there to "hide." After our allotted time in its sacred precincts, we willingly leave and reenter life to face the issues of mortality. But in our hearts we can cherish this experience and cling to the wish that, if we could, we would "dwell in the house of the Lord all the days of my life, to behold the beauty of the Lord." That experience will add to the beauty and joy we can find in every other setting and circumstance.

PSALM 27:10

When my father and my mother forsake me, then the Lord will take me up.

Nothing should be more dependable in a child's life than a mother and father. Fortunately, most parents are magnificent. Even though it may not always be manifest perfectly, the love a father or mother has for a child is the closest thing to divine love that most will ever know in this world. Parenting is so very important for just that reason: as mothers and fathers we represent—and to the best of our ability are to replicate—the love and strength our heavenly parents have for the children they have loaned us. With heavenly parenthood as a backdrop, mortal parenthood takes on its profound, eternal significance.

Unfortunately there is that rare father or mother who abdicates his or her responsibility, who flees home and hearth either literally or figuratively, forsaking the child who looks to that parent for love. That is a painful and devastating thought, but there is evidence of such abandonment in some elements of societies, including societies that make a mockery of marriage and turn a blind eye to the destruction of the family unit. To any child who experiences such a loss—and no child should have to face it—the Psalmist offers an assurance that will never fail, a love that never grows cold, a parenthood that never walks out the door or out of our life. He offers the love of a heavenly parent.

The love of God toward His children is secure. His parenthood is His most treasured role; of all His titles He most prefers that of "Father." He will "take [us] up" in His strong arms when no earthly parent is there to do so. He will *never* forsake us.

PSALMS 30:5; 42:5; 130:6

Weeping may endure for a night, but joy cometh in the morning.

———————

Why art thou cast down, O my soul? and why art thou disquieted in me? hope thou in God.

———————

My soul waiteth for the Lord more than they that watch for the morning.

In a good-natured conversation around the dinner table, the host said that receiving the delightful dessert that had been prepared depended upon his guests' answering a gospel question correctly, namely, "What virtue, what strength is it that no man or woman can live without?"

Guest number one said *faith*—no one could really live without faith in God.

The host replied that faith in God was certainly the most fundamental of religious virtues and that living a truly *good* life or a *saved* life or a *happy* life would certainly require faith. But, no, faith was *not* the answer. Unfortunately, he knew many people who lived without faith in anything and, though that fact was unfortunate, it nevertheless indicated that life could go on without faith because it did for them.

The second guest answered *love*—that no one could really live without love in his or her life.

Again the host qualified the answer, saying that undoubtedly that was true if we were speaking about the love of God, but his question was about virtues *we* have, not that God has. Unfortunately, he said, there were lots of people who lived without love toward anyone or from anyone—and yet they continued to live.

"No," he said in answer to his own question, "I truly believe the most essential ingredient in life and the virtue that lets other blessings like faith and love flourish is *hope*." This doesn't mean that hope is the greatest of the virtues (the Apostle Paul went on record as saying that love was the greatest of these three)[86] but it may mean that in a sense hope is the most essential of the three at least initially, because it can give rise to the other two.

All of us need to believe that things will get better. No matter how dark the night or how long the struggle, we all need to believe that the dawn will come and that the tears of the night will be dried in the rays of the morning sun. The Psalmist is giving us good old-fashioned hope when he promises, "Weeping may endure for a night, but joy cometh in the morning."

Some of our earliest fears in childhood are those in and of the night. Perhaps that is simply an inevitable youthful anxiety. Perhaps it is symbolic of a more theological kind of darkness, a darkness of evil and fear of spiritual destruction. In any case, all of us, whether young or old, have waited through some long nights and looked longingly to the east for the first rays of morning light.

Fortunately, that morning always comes. Fortunately, the

darkness is always driven back and reassurance comes with the sights and sounds of our world coming to life again. Yes, to echo the words of Ecclesiastes, "the sun also ariseth."[87]

How wonderful it would be if we could say with the Psalmist that our soul "waiteth for the Lord more than they that watch for the morning." We ought to anticipate the Savior's light in our life as anxiously as we hope for the warmth and rising of that reassuring sun. Christ is the "bright and morning star"[88]—the sun/Son. One day He will come again to rule and reign as Lord of Lords and King of Kings. For that day we eagerly and longingly wait "more than they that watch for the morning."

In the course of living there are plenty of chances for weeping. But those tears are not permanent; that despair is not endless. In the dark of the night, in the midst of our troubles, we may not see any way out or any reprieve to come, but that feeling passes as the night passes. Things will get better in the morning. With the dawning of a new day (or the day after that, or the day after that) joy will return. It may not come as soon as we would like in every case. Relief might not initially be as recognizable as we would like it to be, but it comes nevertheless. No matter how much weeping endures for a night, there will always be joy in the morning if we "hope . . . in God."

PSALMS 31:12; 34:18; 51:10, 17

I am like a broken vessel.

The Lord is nigh unto them that are of a broken heart; and saveth such as be of a contrite spirit.

Create in me a clean heart, O God; and renew a right spirit within me. . . .

The sacrifices of God are a broken spirit: a broken and a contrite heart, O God, thou wilt not despise.

Sometimes the events of life can damage our highest hopes and dreams. Some of our sweetest possessions and most cherished ideals end up being bruised, and sometimes they are broken. In the world of items we treasure we may break a lovely piece of china or a pocket watch handed down from an ancestor. Sometimes even bones break, and even more painfully, marriages or family ties are broken. In severed circumstances we truly feel "like a broken vessel"; we are certain that, as with Humpty Dumpty, all the king's horses and all the king's men will never be able to put us together again.

But someone wrote once that God apparently loves—and turns to our benefit—broken things. It takes broken clouds to nourish the earth, it takes broken earth to grow grain, it takes broken grain to make bread, it takes broken bread to nourish us, and so are the cycles of life. This divine sequence is akin to the Savior's parable that no kernel of corn can grow to fruition until it is first thrown away and, in effect, lost in the earth before its bounty can come back to us.[89]

So it is with broken hearts and contrite spirits. We must remember that the children of God are still under covenant to sacrifice. However, we do not offer the firstlings of the flock or the initial harvest from the vineyard anymore. No, with the coming of Christ, that kind of sacrifice was put to an end and we were commanded to offer newer symbols of Christ's Atonement: "Thou shalt offer a sacrifice unto the Lord thy God in righteousness, even that of a broken heart and a contrite spirit."[90]

It may be that among all the broken things God loves, He loves a broken heart most of all. So when our day of sacrifice comes—and perhaps sorrow will come with it—be trusting and be believing. Know that God will accept your offering and that, through the great miracle of the Atonement of Jesus Christ, He will give your heart back to you healed and whole. That is the ultimate truth taught by the Resurrection. Christ, the Great Healer, will make recompense for us in time and in eternity. By His grace and the goodness of God, all broken vessels are fully repaired.

PSALM 32:7

Thou art my hiding place; thou shalt preserve me from trouble; thou shalt compass me about with songs of deliverance.

I am not a musician, but I love music. I have the good fortune to be married to a magnificent musician. She has made music an inextricable part of our home and a constant in our life. Furthermore, it has been my experience in Church administration that nothing brings the Spirit of the Lord to a meeting more powerfully than good music, "songs of deliverance," if you will. One of the early pieces of advice I had as a General Authority was that "we ought to have great music in the Church and more of it, coupled with great speaking in the Church and less of it."

Music has not only the charm "to soothe a savage breast, to soften rocks, or bend a knotted oak,"[91] but it has also the power to edify and exalt the spirit that is already elevated. Indeed, I think we could postulate that the more refined the spirit is, the greater impact good music has on it. And when we are in difficulty, nothing can quite touch our heart like a melody that seems to have been sent directly from heaven. It has been said—and I personally believe it is true—that in the compendium of sacred expression in the Church, the hymns of

Zion take their rightful place following the scriptures and the teachings of the living prophets. Whether it is the grandeur of a marvelous Tabernacle Choir performance or the heartfelt musical testimony from a frightened soloist in the most distant unit of the Church, the "songs of deliverance" have always been an encouragement to the troubled, a comfort to those who are burdened. It should not surprise us that when *both* trouble and burdens faced our pioneer ancestors, they sang, "Gird up your loins, fresh courage take. Our God will never us forsake; and soon we'll have this tale to tell—all is well! All is well!"[92] We thank the Lord for good music of every kind—from folk ballads to Bach and Beethoven to the hymns of Zion. We rejoice in melody, in harmony, in orchestrated eloquence that "songs of deliverance" employ in speaking to the soul.

Apparently the Savior of the world understood the great blessing of music as well, for in His hour of eternal "deliverance," He introduced the sacrament of the Lord's Supper, sang a hymn with His brethren, and moved resolutely toward the sorrow of Gethsemane and the pain of Calvary.[93] We would all like to believe that singing that hymn provided additional strength for this most troubling moment in human history. Uplifting music can do the same for us in our times of need.

PSALM 34:7

The angel of the Lord encampeth round about them that fear him, and delivereth them.

However much we believe in angels, we ought to believe in them more than we do, for they truly do "[encamp] round about" us and they regularly protect and deliver us in many different ways. From ancient times to modern, the ministry of angels has been one of the principal ways God has communicated with, watched over, and given both physical and spiritual safety to His children on earth. An angel was sent to comfort and counsel Adam and Eve when they were newly driven out of the Garden of Eden.[94] Thereafter a host of angels delivered various messages and gave varied service down through Old Testament times until, when the Savior's advent was at hand, the angel Gabriel was sent first to Zacharias to announce the birth of the messianic forerunner, John the Baptist, and then to Mary to declare she was to be the mother of the Son of God.[95] Following this message to Mary, an angel (Gabriel again?) conveyed all this wondrous information to Joseph and told him to take Mary as his wife.

After the baby's birth, an angel warned Joseph that the newborn was in danger and the family must flee to Egypt for safety. Later yet, an angel conveyed that it was safe to return to the land of their family's heritage.[96] And this was only the beginning of Jesus' life. Angels seen and unseen would watch over Him, and on occasion attend to Him, as He carried out the mission given Him by His Father in Heaven in fulfilling the plan for our salvation and working out the Atonement for the sins of all mankind.[97]

Although Jesus' life and mission were precious and special by every standard, nevertheless we also have the watchcare and attention of angels from on high. More than three hundred times the scriptures refer to angelic visitations, ministrations, and interventions to a wide variety of people, often very common people. And these are only those examples that have been canonized! How many times have individual men, women, and children seen or heard or been attended to by angels in circumstances that are not scriptural, but are in effect the everyday experiences of everyday lives? Occasionally there are divine manifestations allowing us to behold the angelic presence among us, but usually these heavenly agents come and go and in our innocence we "entertained [them] unawares."[98]

We have referred to the angels who attended the birth of Jesus, experiences that get rehearsed each year at Christmastime. However, perhaps if our eyes were more spiritually keen and our ears more heavenly attuned, we might well be able to sing throughout the year, "Hark, the Herald Angels Sing" or, "Angels We Have Heard on High," for surely they are there and are watching over us.

"Has the day of miracles ceased? Or have angels ceased to appear unto the children of men? Or has he withheld the power of the Holy Ghost from them? Or will he, so long as time shall last, or the earth shall stand, or there shall be one man upon the face thereof to be saved? Behold I say unto you, Nay; for . . . it is by faith that angels appear and minister unto men. . . . For behold, they are subject unto [Christ], to minister according to the word of his command, showing

PSALM 34:7

The angel of the Lord encampeth round about them that fear him, and delivereth them.

themselves unto them of strong faith and a firm mind in every form of godliness."[99]

Keep a strong faith and a firm mind. The angels of the Lord will encamp round about you and deliver you.

PSALM 36:9

For with thee is the fountain of life: in thy light shall we see light.

Darkness is so often literally or metaphorically the enemy. Lucifer is considered the prince of darkness, and hell itself is portrayed as a dark and dismal setting, a place in which there is literally no light. Sometimes our mortal lives are so difficult that it feels hope has fled and we are left to stumble on in darkness.

How important it is early in our lives, then, for us to learn that in the light of God, the light of Christ, the light of the Spirit, not only will we experience light itself, but it shall be the source of illumination for everything else upon which we gaze.

The redemptive role of the light of Christ is an important doctrine in the restored gospel.[100] We believe that every single individual born into this world carries and keeps that light in his or her soul, no matter what time or transgression might do in an attempt to extinguish it. It *cannot* be fully extinguished. If we give that light a chance, it will be the means of seeing light. It will grow to become the everlasting light by which all men, women, and children can recognize the truth, respond to it, and make covenants with the Lord.

After this world in which we so much need pure and true light to help us find our way and read the meaning in things, kingdoms of glory await us that are symbolically characterized by additional degrees of light—the light of the stars, the light of the moon, and, ultimately the brightest of all, the light of the sun.[101] Indeed the light surrounding the Father and the Son was described by the Prophet Joseph Smith as being "*above* the brightness of the sun."[102]

If you have fears about loved ones who are currently darkened, hope on. The light emanating from "the fountain of life" quickens that corresponding light in each of us if we will but allow it to do so. I have felt darkness and pled for redeeming light. It has always come— surely, steadily, eventually.

"He is the light and the life of the world; yea, a light that is endless, that can never be darkened."[103] By His light we still see light— and can walk in it—forever.

PSALMS 37:16; 49:16–17; 73:3

A little that a righteous man hath is better than the riches of many wicked.

Be not thou afraid when one is made rich, when the glory of his house is increased;

For when he dieth he shall carry nothing away: his glory shall not descend after him.

For I was envious at the foolish, when I saw the prosperity of the wicked.

Adam and Eve were told when they left the Garden of Eden that they would be required to earn their living by the sweat of their brow. We have all been sweating ever since, some with more success than others. The history of humankind down through the ages has been the history of men and women striving to acquire enough goods of this world to sustain their lives and protect their children.

If a question were asked of the average man or woman on the street, "What causes you the most stress in your life?" it is entirely possible that he or she would answer, "Finances—how to acquire them, how to use them, how to save them, and in some cases how not to let them destroy us."

We all yearn for the day when there are no poor among us, when every man, woman, and child will have sufficient economic and temporal blessings to meet their needs. That is a worthy community goal to strive for. It is one of the principal Zion-like characteristics of perfect societal living. We may not achieve that standard until the great millennial day under Christ's personal rule, but we can strive for it.

In the meantime, we should do everything we can to reduce the stress that finances impose on our lives. We should prepare ourselves for provident living the best way we can, with all the education and training we can get to facilitate that. In the process we need to curb our appetites, not to spend more than we make, not to want more than we need, and not to think we need more than we really do. It is a cliché—but true nevertheless—to note how little of this world's goods people need to be happy and, conversely, how many unhappy people have a great deal of this world's goods. Again, that is not to be cavalier toward those who are truly poor—true poverty may do more to destroy the human spirit than any other condition except sin itself. And how doubly tragic if the circumstances of poverty lead to sin. Money for its own sake—more and more of this and more and more of that—has since the beginning of time proven to be not only insufficient for happiness but sometimes a countering force against it.

Strive to live within your means. No one can keep up with the Joneses because the Joneses are going to refinance. Be modest, save regularly, pay tithes and offerings, help the poor. Live with the peace that comes from the righteous use of money.

Jacob in the Book of Mormon said we would have riches if we sought to do wisely with them. "Think of your brethren like unto yourselves," he said, "and be familiar with all and free with your substance, that they may be rich like unto you. But before ye seek for riches, seek ye for the kingdom of God. And after ye have obtained a hope in Christ ye shall obtain riches, if ye seek them; and ye will seek them for the intent to do good—to clothe the naked, and to feed the hungry, and to liberate the captive, and administer relief to the sick and the afflicted."[104] For most of us, those riches won't be excessive. Some days it will seem they are hardly even sufficient. But if we live in righteousness, they will be. "A little that a righteous man hath is better than the riches of many wicked."

One other related thought: Perhaps there is nothing more ironic than that otherwise intelligent, honest people would envy what foolish people have or would yearn for that which has been acquired by wicked means. Name two categories of people we would least like to be associated with or compared to and surely "the foolish" and "the wicked" would be at the top of the list. Why do we then spend time, money, or emotion envying what is not admirable or trying to become like people with whom we don't really want to associate? Jesus said, "By their fruits ye shall know them."[105] Does it not follow that foolish possessions reveal foolish people or, worse yet, that evil practices reveal wicked people and sinister motives? Alexander Pope wrote that "to err is human,"[106] and that is probably so, but surely to *want* what is in error, to envy it and long for it and lust after it, is *in*human—or at least unworthy.

But more serious here than what is envied is envy itself. One of the cardinal commandments marking the Judeo-Christian world for four millennia has been "Thou shalt not covet."[107] In some ways it seems the saddest, the most pathetic, of all the Ten Commandments. That is because envy is usually not about what we lack but rather is an anger (or at the very least a resentment) about what someone else has. In short, it is truly petty—a way of thinking directed not at all toward building up ourselves but toward tearing someone else down. We can avoid a lot of sorrow and disappointment if we learn to envy less, enjoy what we do have more, and give to those who truly need it.

PSALM 37:23–24

The steps of a good man are ordered by the Lord: and he delighteth in his way.

Though he fall, he shall not be utterly cast down: for the Lord upholdeth him with his hand.

Note that this psalm speaks of "a good man" whose steps are sanctioned by heaven and pleasing to all. And yet even he (or she), as well as the habitual sinner, may have a moment of falling from safety and sure footing.

Surely a most encouraging truth in the gospel of Jesus Christ is contained in the thought that though *any* man fall—good or bad—"he shall not be utterly cast down: for the Lord upholdeth him with his hand." That is the essence of the "good news" Jesus came to declare. Mistakes can be overcome, sins can be forgiven, death is not the victor, and hell is not our destiny. Everything that Christ and the prophets taught comes back to this truth that through desire and obedience all can be forgiven of sins. Everything that could have been can yet be—and more.

Sometimes we might think we are the only one who has ever

stumbled or fallen and might understandably ask, "How could this have happened to me?" But only one man in all the history of this world was perfect. All others "have sinned, and come short of the glory of God."[108] However, just because that scripture reassures us that there is a lot of company in the circle of transgressors, this should never be an excuse to accept poor behavior or justify our sins. It should, rather, be encouraging to know that everyone—good *or* bad—is working to recover from some kind of shortcoming, and in such an effort there is divine help for every one of us.

Fortunately, most of those "falls" are small missteps. But some can be very serious. Whether great or small, short- or long-term, the promise is nevertheless the same. If we are trying to be good—or if we are trying to be good again after a period when we weren't—those steps to recovery are "ordered by the Lord" and He does delight in our way. Nothing touches the deepest chamber of a parent's heart more than a son's or daughter's effort to return to them and return to God. No parent can live with the thought that there is no hope, that his or her child is "utterly cast down," with no helping hand to uphold.

Fortunately, as always in the gospel of Jesus Christ, there is a hand extended. It is never withdrawn. It is always there.

PSALM 40:10

I have not hid thy righteousness within my heart; I have declared thy faithfulness and thy salvation: I have not concealed thy lovingkindness and thy truth from the great congregation.

We have always had a fundamental obligation in the gospel of Jesus Christ to share that "good news" with others. When we have been blessed with some redeeming truth or have been given some spiritual insight, the call is always to share it. When in his dream Lehi saw the great tree of life and experienced the delicious fruit thereof—more delicious than anything else in the world—his immediate instinct was to turn and look for his family.[109] When Enos had poured out his soul in prayer and received a remarkable, redeeming promise from God, his response was to continue praying, asking for such a blessing to come to others.[110] When we see a stunning rainbow or a spectacular sunset, we are anxious for others—especially our loved ones—to see it with us. When we have had an exciting holiday or taken a trip to a lovely place, we send back photos or postcards to convey the delight we have felt and how much we want others to share in our pleasure.

That is the way we are expected to be about the righteousness

God demonstrates and the lovingkindness He shows to us. We could call it missionary work, but that becomes a somewhat trite phrase. It is more an appreciation of what we have been given and a desire to share what makes life so rewarding. It is seeing ourselves as an instrument for teaching the love God has for us and for declaring the blessings He so willingly pours out upon His children.

When we have received such blessings, let us not conceal them from "the great congregation." We would not want to hide God's righteousness so privately. The prophet Alma said that we should carry the image of Christ in our countenances.[111] In short, we ought to look like we are happy, like we are blessed, like we are recipients of the truth—and then live, speak, and share accordingly. Our greatest missionary message is our own righteous lives, our own buoyant happiness, our own willing speech testifying of good things given to us so freely.

PSALM 41:1

Blessed is he that considereth the poor: the Lord will deliver him in time of trouble.

Surely God has no greater concern for any than He has for the poor, the destitute, the impoverished. It would seem that no other sound ascends to His ears more readily and more painfully than "the sighing of the needy."[112]

Even in the strict day of the Mosaic code, the Lord commanded that if someone lent money to those who were poor, the borrowers were not to be charged any interest. In the six years that the Israelite fields and farms were producing, the owner was not to glean them in order that the poor might glean there and eat. Then every seventh year the fields were to be entirely free to the needy for the full twelve months, "that the poor of thy people may eat."[113]

Consider this small sample of the myriad scriptural injunctions given in defense of the poor:

He raiseth up the poor out of the dust, and lifteth up the beggar from the dunghill, to set them among princes, and to make them inherit the throne of glory: for the pillars of the earth are the Lord's, and he hath set the world upon them.[114]

Whoso mocketh the poor reproacheth his Maker: and he that is glad at calamities shall not be unpunished.[115]

He that giveth unto the poor shall not lack: but he that hideth his eyes shall have many a curse.[116]

Jesus said unto him, If thou wilt be perfect, go and sell that thou hast, and give to the poor, and thou shalt have treasure in heaven: and come and follow me.[117]

For behold, are we not all beggars? Do we not all depend upon the same Being, even God, for all the substance which we have, for both food and raiment, and for gold, and for silver, and for all the riches which we have of every kind?[118]

And now, for the sake of these things which I have spoken unto you—that is, for the sake of retaining a remission of your sins from day to day, that ye may walk guiltless before God—I would that ye should impart of your substance to the poor, every man according to that which he hath, such as feeding the hungry, clothing the naked, visiting the sick and administering to their relief, both spiritually and temporally, according to their wants.[119]

And they did impart of their substance, every man according to that which he had, to the poor, and the needy, and the sick, and the afflicted; and they did not wear costly apparel, yet they were neat and comely.[120]

———————

[They] were abasing themselves, succoring those who stood in need of their succor, such as imparting their substance to the poor and the needy, feeding the hungry, and suffering all manner of afflictions, for Christ's sake, who should come according to the spirit of prophecy.[121]

———————

Yea, and will you persist in turning your backs upon the poor, and the needy, and in withholding your substance from them?[122]

———————

If ye turn away the needy, and the naked, and visit not the sick and afflicted, and impart of your substance, if ye have, to those who stand in need—I say unto you, if ye do not any of these things, behold, your prayer is vain, and availeth you nothing, and ye are as hypocrites who do deny the faith.[123]

———————

For behold, ye do love money, and your substance, and your fine apparel, and the adorning of your churches, more than ye love the poor and the needy, the sick and the afflicted.[124]

———————

And inasmuch as ye impart of your substance unto the poor, ye will do it unto me.[125]

——————

But behold, they have not learned to be obedient to the things which I required at their hands, but are full of all manner of evil, and do not impart of their substance, as becometh saints, to the poor and afflicted among them.[126]

——————

Perhaps nothing so crushes the human spirit as does poverty. May it never be said of us that we "beat [God's] people to pieces, and [did] grind the faces of the poor."[127] Truly the Lord will deliver, in time of his or her trouble, the man or woman who has reached out to the poor in theirs.

PSALM 55:16–17

As for me, I will call upon God; and the Lord shall save me.

Evening, and morning, and at noon, will I pray, and cry aloud: and he shall hear my voice.

One of our scriptures equates prayer with the purest, simplest form of worship.[128] In mortality, whether it be from the safe space of a child's cradle or in our gray-haired final moments, the closest, most private and personal relationship we have with God is in solitary, single-minded prayer.

The scriptures say that we should "pray always,"[129] however demanding that invitation may seem. Obviously, one cannot always be offering a formal prayer or a kneeling prayer or even a vocal prayer, but we can have a prayer in our heart at all times and have our longing be fixed upon the Lord. Amulek phrases it as "let[ting] your hearts be full, drawn out in prayer unto him continually."[130] Alma said to his son Helaman, "Let all thy thoughts be directed unto the Lord; yea, let the affections of thy heart be placed upon the Lord forever."[131]

But having said that about a prayerful heart and heaven-oriented

PSALM 55:16–17

As for me, I will call upon God; and the Lord shall save me.

Evening, and morning, and at noon, will I pray, and cry aloud: and he shall hear my voice.

attitude, it must be acknowledged that God also expects us to actually "cry aloud," to have honest, earnest vocal prayer on a regular basis. To pray "evening, and morning, and at noon" is evidence of the Psalmist's obedience to this command. Not that the prayers of our heart should ever be formulated or numbered, but it is interesting to note how often in the scriptures the ancients prayed in a formal way at least three times a day. The Book of Mormon records the injunction to "cry unto him in your houses, yea, over all your household, both morning, mid-day, and evening,"[132] and the courageous Daniel "kneeled upon his knees three times a day, and prayed."[133]

We should not get mechanical in our prayer habits. The number of times we pray is much less important than the earnestness and faith with which those prayers are offered. But there is a constant reminder in the scriptures to pray always, to let prayer mark the way we start our day, the way we pursue our day, and the way we conclude our day.

Why? Beyond the fact that God is our Father and we need His loving, omniscient guidance always, there are repeated reminders in the scriptures that there is a particular safety in prayer, a special protection from evil. And since evil is always "abroad in the land,"[134] the counsel we find in holy writ says that we should pray always "lest [we] enter into temptation."[135] Inherent in that counsel may be the simple recognition that a prayerful, humble person is less likely to go seeking for trouble, to go where evil influence is likely to be. But this call to prayer undoubtedly means a great deal more than that—that there is literally divine protection in prayer, a shield, if you will (a favorite word in the psalms), which in response to the humble prayer of the faithful keeps evil at bay and forbids the forces of Lucifer from overpowering us.

We should always have a prayer in our hearts and, as often as practicable, we should "cry aloud" to our Father in Heaven. There is power in the articulation of prayerful words, the sound they have in our own ears as well as the sound that they carry to heaven.

In seasons of distress and grief
My soul has often found relief
And oft escaped the tempter's snare
By thy return, sweet hour of prayer.[136]

PSALMS 57:7; 26:1–2, 11

My heart is fixed, O God, my heart is fixed.

Judge me, O Lord; for I have walked in mine integrity. . . .

Examine me, O Lord, and prove me; try my reins and my heart. . . .

I will walk in mine integrity.

When difficulties are upon us and when trouble seems everywhere, part of the endurance spoken of so often in the psalms is characterized here as being "fixed." When we have done all else we can do, we can take our stand, plant our feet, stiffen our resolve, and fix our heart. As a great religious reformer once said, so we can say: "I stand here and can say no more. God help me."[137]

We can't always control external experiences. We can't always control the forces of nature or mortality. Things swirl around us coming from the complexity of telestial life that won't always yield to our wishes. But we can fix our heart. We can remain true, we can keep our integrity, we can hold to that which we believe. No matter what happens, we can refuse to be dissuaded in our faith or altered in our loyalty to God and true principles.

Job, the archetype for the tried and troubled man, said even as his woes mounted and his ills increased: "All the while my breath is in me, and the spirit of God is in my nostrils; my lips shall not speak wickedness, nor my tongue utter deceit. God forbid that I should justify you: till I die I will not remove mine integrity from me. . . . Let me be weighed in an even balance, that God may know mine integrity."[138]

But what do we do if we are not always as strong as Job? Where do we turn for greater integrity than our own, for determination to be true when we are stumbling? One of the wonderful hymns that we sing about the Atonement reminds us how we can fix our heart—or, more properly, *who* can fix our heart—when we are not as firm as we ought to be:

> *O to grace how great a debtor*
> *Daily I'm constrained to be!*
> *Let thy goodness, as a fetter,*
> *Bind my wandering heart to thee.*
> *Prone to wander, Lord, I feel it,*
> *Prone to leave the God I love;*
> *Here's my heart; O, take and seal it;*
> *Seal it for thy courts above.*[139]

However weak or tried or tempted we may feel, Christ can seal us, fix us, fasten us "as a nail in a sure place."[140] His gift to us was fixed with just such certainty on the cross at Calvary.

PSALM 61:2

From the end of the earth will I cry unto thee, when my heart is overwhelmed: lead me to the rock that is higher than I.

When the floods of trouble swirl around us, our most obvious need is to find a sure, safe place on higher ground. That is what the gospel of Jesus Christ offers every man, woman, and child. When Peter and John were hastening into the temple shortly after the Savior's Crucifixion, Resurrection, and ascension into heaven, a beggar called out to them from the steps of the temple, asking for an alms. The scriptures say that he was a man crippled from his birth who had spent nearly forty years of his life being carried to and from these temple steps where he could beg of those going into the house of the Lord.

When he saw Peter and John, he made his appeal of them. These two Apostles, former fishermen who had left their nets to follow the Savior, had no material wealth of any kind. Peter said to the man, "Look on us." And the man looked on him, expecting to receive an alms. Peter then said, "Silver and gold have I none; but such as I have give I thee: In the name of Jesus Christ of Nazareth rise up and walk."

And then the passage says, "And he took him by the right hand, and lifted him up."[141]

President Harold B. Lee said of that experience: "Will you see that picture now of that noble soul, that chiefest of the apostles, perhaps with his arms around the shoulders of this man, and saying, 'Now, my good man, have courage, I will take a few steps with you. Let's walk together, and I assure you that you can walk, because you have received a blessing by the power and authority that God has given us as men, his servants.'" Then President Lee said to his audience, "You cannot lift another soul until you are standing on higher ground than he is. You must be sure, if you would rescue the man, that you yourself are setting the example of what you would have him be."[142]

All of us have days when we are "overwhelmed," days of meekness and lowliness of heart. In such times all of us cry out for someone—anyone—to lead us to higher ground, to more stable footing. How grateful we are to those who are strong and faithful, those who reach down, lift others up, and set them on the rock of Christ. In those times we give thanks to heaven for all helpers—and He who is our ultimate help always, who not only stands on high ground but *is* high ground, who not only raises us to a rock but *is* that rock.

PSALM 69:3

I am weary of my crying . . .

This brief line needs no real commentary. It speaks eloquently enough in its six-word poignancy. Surely every one of us has had some sorrow, some intensely personal grief so great that we became weary simply shedding so many tears. When these times come, it may help to remember three things:

First, a good cry is therapeutic. No one wants this kind of therapy too often, but it is true that the release of such powerful, pent-up emotion can be good for us. In deeply personal circumstances it is both natural and appropriate to weep, to let some equilibrium come back and restore our emotional balance.

Second, one of the greatest of all scenes recorded in latter-day scripture is the description of Enoch's encounter with God wherein our Father in Heaven is seen weeping over His children on earth.

"And it came to pass that the God of heaven looked upon the residue of the people, and he wept, . . . And Enoch said unto the Lord: How is it that thou canst weep, seeing thou art holy, and from all eternity to all eternity? . . . The Lord said unto Enoch: Behold these thy brethren; they are the workmanship of mine own hands, . . . the whole heavens shall weep over them . . . wherefore should not the heavens weep, seeing these shall suffer?"[143] Christ also wept for the sorrows and troubles of His people.[144] If divine beings can weep over the ills and sorrows to be faced in mortality,[145] so can we.

Third, what comfort we take from the promise of another psalm, "They that sow in tears shall reap in joy."[146] Sometimes (we hope not too often) the only way to reap joy is to sow tears. There may be pain, effort, hard work, and sorrow in bearing, planting, and sowing precious seed, but the promises of the Lord are sure: "Whatsoever ye sow, that shall ye also reap."[147] And every one of us can trust that someday, somehow, somewhere every good seed we have sown and every honest deed we have done, every faithful effort we have made and every virtuous thought we have had will bring its own reward and will be counted for our good in the great days of divine harvest.

When you are weary from crying, hold on. Those tears will soon be dried from your eyes.

PSALM 71:9, 18

Cast me not off in the time of old age; forsake me not when my strength faileth. . . .

Now also when I am old and grayheaded, O God, forsake me not; until I have shewed thy strength unto this generation, and thy power to every one that is to come.

When we are young, there is a wonderful temptation to think we are immortal, invincible, that the future is ours and we will always be healthy and strong. To a child there are precious few thoughts of growing old, much less moving toward true infirmity. But then the years take their toll, decades pass, and in the end finally our "strength faileth."

Because there are lessons to be learned in our old age that simply are not possible in our youth, God intended us to know the full range of mortal experience. As Ralph Waldo Emerson once wrote, "The years teach much which the days never know."[148]

Unfortunately, with old age can come genuine disability—disease, disappointment, limited use of our bodies, and sometimes limited use of our minds. Probably every "senior citizen" has had an occasion to say to the Lord, "Cast me not off in the time of old age; forsake me not when my strength faileth."

But added to that general plea for help in such times ought to be a special plea still to show God's strength "unto this generation." We want not to fall short because often we have not yet fulfilled our missions. We have not yet demonstrated all of the power and strength of the gospel that has made us what we are and shaped our lives into what we are yet trying to become. The younger generation—our children and our children's children—need to see that in us and hear it from our lips. There are lessons the elderly have learned that can only be learned—and can only be taught—by the elderly. We can't glean them from any other source in any other way.

So to all those who are feeling "old and grayheaded," we say hold on, pray on, keep living and loving and learning. And above all, keep teaching. Find every opportunity to teach the next generation all that God has done for you, all the faith—and the miracles coming from it—that you have seen in your lifetime. Perhaps your greatest sermon will be the eloquence of your long and worthy life. Celebrate even the aged season of your life and pray that it might be extended "until [you] have shewed [heaven's] strength unto this generation, and [God's] power to every one that is to come."

PSALM 77:10–12

I will remember the years of the right hand of the most High.

I will remember the works of the Lord: surely I will remember thy wonders of old.

I will meditate also of all thy work, and talk of thy doings.

When difficult times come and continue with us for a while, it can begin to feel that life has always been difficult, that we have never been happy, that we can't remember ever being blessed. But that is grossly unfair to ourselves and to God. Of course we have been happy. Of course we have been blessed. Times are not always difficult, and when trials come we can get past them more quickly if we remember happiness in the past as readily as we count on the promise of happiness ahead.

Everything about the gospel of Jesus Christ is ultimately directed toward the joy for which we came to this earth[149] and the "perfect brightness of hope"[150] we are to have as we pursue future glory in eternity. Ours is ultimately a "plan of happiness,"[151] even though not every moment in it is necessarily a happy one. But there is regular happiness in it, and certainly there is happiness at the end of the journey. So, it is not only good advice, it is a moral obligation to "remember the years of the right hand of the most High." We owe it to God and to ourselves to "remember the works of the Lord . . . [with their] wonders of old." It is not surprising that a favorite Christian hymn gives that same counsel:

> *When upon life's billows you are tempest tossed,*
> *When you are discouraged, thinking all is lost,*
> *Count your many blessings; name them one by one,*
> *And it will surprise you what the Lord has done.*[152]

But notice that the psalm counsels us to do something more than passively remember or mindlessly enumerate. It counsels us to "*meditate* [upon] all [God's] work, and *talk* of [all His] doings." Both of these activities—meditating upon and talking about the goodness of God—are among the greatest of self-help steps we can take to heal a troubled heart. Thinking about God—about His nature, His love, His compassion, His blessings to us—is in and of itself a spiritual experience. These are powerful thoughts, and they drive out negative feelings and sad memories. Talking about these blessings—in effect, "bearing our testimony" about them even if only to ourselves or to those close to us—fixes those spiritual feelings in our hearts and gives them an objective existence of their own. To verbalize something is to give it life,[153] so when we speak of our blessings aloud, the reality of them becomes more obvious, more powerful, more permanent.

When troubles come, remember the right hand of the most High. Remember the wonders of old. Meditate upon your blessings—talk of them—"one by one." And remember Amulek's counsel: "Live in thanksgiving daily, for the many mercies and blessings which [God] doth bestow upon you."[154]

PSALMS 78:5–8; 145:4

He established a testimony in Jacob, and appointed a law in Israel, which he commanded our fathers, that they should make them known to their children:

That the generation to come might know them, even the children which should be born; who should arise and declare them to their children:

That they might set their hope in God, and not forget the works of God, but keep his commandments:

And might not be as their fathers, a stubborn and rebellious generation; a generation that set not their heart aright, and whose spirit was not stedfast with God.

One generation shall praise thy works to another, and shall declare thy mighty acts.

One of the great commandments to ancient Israel (and to the contemporary Church) is to pass on to the next generation a record and a testimony of the teachings of God—His blessings, His commandments, His covenants, His miracles. All fathers and mothers are to make these things known to their children. This is so "that the generation to come might know them, even the children which should be born," and they, in turn, would teach "their children"—the grandchildren, as it were—that all the generations might set their hopes on God and keep His commandments.

The backdrop drama of Lehi's and Sariah's descendants in the Book of Mormon is a classic example of some fathers failing to pass on to their children correct truths and saving traditions. Much of the loss suffered by the Lamanite people in that book is due to the fact that the younger generations in those families either were not taught at all or were taught the false traditions of their parents. Later in the book that becomes equally true of some portions of the Nephite family. The warning of the psalm (and of the Book of Mormon) is clear: we are to teach the next generation and those that are yet unborn, that they "might not be as their fathers, a stubborn and rebellious generation; a generation that set not their heart aright, and whose spirit was not stedfast with God."[155]

We are reminded that when Joshua was leading the children of Israel to the promised land and was miraculously allowed to cross the river on dry ground, he said to those who had lived the miracle: "Take ye up every man of you a stone upon his shoulder, according unto the number of the tribes of the children of Israel: That this may be a sign among you, that when your children ask their fathers in time to come, saying, What mean ye by these stones? Then ye shall answer them, That the waters of Jordan were cut off before the ark of the covenant of the Lord; when it passed over Jordan, the waters of Jordan were cut off: and these stones shall be for a memorial unto the children of Israel for ever."[156] That is only one example of one generation leaving a testimony to a future generation about the wonders of God and His "mighty acts" in their lives.

Toward the end of his life, Nephi said that the things he had written were to be "kept and preserved, and handed down unto my seed, from generation to generation. . . . Wherefore, these things shall go from generation to generation as long as the earth shall stand. . . . For we labor diligently to write, to persuade our children, and also our brethren, to believe in Christ, and to be reconciled to God; for we know that it is by grace that we are saved, after all we can do. . . . Wherefore, we speak . . . that our children may know the deadness of the law; and they, by knowing the deadness of the law, may look forward unto that life which is in Christ."[157]

We ought to bear testimony often. We certainly ought to bear testimony to those who have not heard what we have heard and seen what we have seen. Among those several audiences, no group deserves to hear the testimony, receive the stories, and hear of our convictions more than our own children.

PSALM 85:11

Truth shall spring out of the earth; and righteousness shall look down from heaven.

To everyone in The Church of Jesus Christ of Latter-day Saints, this line ought to have a wonderfully familiar ring to it. In the seventh chapter of the book of Moses in the Pearl of Great Price, the Lord speaks of the last days, saying, "And . . . the heavens shall be darkened, and a veil of darkness shall cover the earth; and the heavens shall shake, and also the earth; and great tribulations shall be among the children of men." But then this wonderfully reassuring promise, "But my people will I preserve."[158] How will He preserve them? He will preserve them by restoring the gospel of Jesus Christ. Predating the prophecy of Psalm 85:11, the Lord says of such latter-day troubled times, "And righteousness will I send down out of heaven; and truth will I send forth out of the earth, to bear testimony of mine Only Begotten; his resurrection from the dead; yea, and also the resurrection of all men; and righteousness and truth will I cause to sweep the earth as with a flood, to gather out mine elect from the four quarters of the earth."[159]

Obviously so very much that we enjoy in the restored gospel of

Jesus Christ features truth that sprang out of the earth in the form of the Book of Mormon and righteousness that has looked down from heaven in the form of divine visitations and recurring revelations. The Father and the Son appeared to the boy prophet and ushered in the greatest of all dispensations—*our* dispensation. The angel Moroni came to restore "another testament of Jesus Christ"—the Book of Mormon. Ancient prophets and apostles left heaven to visit the earth and restore priesthood keys, including keys for the gathering of Israel from across the earth, keys of the dispensation of Abraham through whom all the families of that grand patriarch will be blessed, keys employed in all priesthood work, including the temple, by which the hearts of the fathers would turn to the children and the hearts of the children would turn to the fathers. The story of the restored gospel is a long, happy sequence of eternal truth springing out of the earth and continual righteousness coming down from heaven. Little wonder the Prophet Joseph Smith would cry out in poetic zeal:

"Shall we not go on in so great a cause? . . . Let the mountains shout for joy, and all ye valleys cry aloud; and all ye seas and dry lands tell the wonders of your Eternal King! And ye rivers, and brooks, and rills, flow down with gladness. Let the woods and all the trees of the field praise the Lord; and ye solid rocks weep for joy! And let the sun, moon, and the morning stars sing together, and let all the sons of God shout for joy! And let the eternal creations declare his name forever and ever! And again I say, how glorious is the voice we hear from heaven, proclaiming in our ears, glory, and salvation, and honor, and immortality, and eternal life; kingdoms, principalities, and powers!"[160]

PSALMS 86:3–6; 103:8–11, 17–18; 119:58

Be merciful unto me, O Lord: for I cry unto thee daily.

Rejoice the soul of thy servant: for unto thee, O Lord, do I lift up my soul.

For thou, Lord, art good, and ready to forgive; and plenteous in mercy unto all them that call upon thee.

Give ear, O Lord, unto my prayer; and attend to the voice of my supplications.

The Lord is merciful and gracious, slow to anger, and plenteous in mercy.

He will not always chide: neither will he keep his anger for ever.

He hath not dealt with us after our sins; nor rewarded us according to our iniquities.

For as the heaven is high above the earth, so great is his mercy toward them that fear him. . . .

But the mercy of the Lord is from everlasting to everlasting upon them that fear him, and his righteousness unto children's children;

To such as keep his covenant, and to those that remember his commandments to do them.

I intreated thy favour with my whole heart: be merciful unto me according to thy word.

One of the unfortunate legacies of traditional Christianity in an earlier era is the image of a wrathful, vengeful, angry God who is something like a mean-spirited umpire who is anxious to call us out on strikes in baseball or give us a red card in soccer. What a tragedy this is and what a heartbreak it must be to Him who is the Father of us all.

Obviously our Father in Heaven has expectations for us and can be disappointed with our actions. With severe transgression He can be genuinely angry, the way any loving parent might be angry at the foolishness or dangerous choices of a child, but He is very slow to anger and He will not "keep his anger for ever." Above all, He is merciful, and that is because He is good. He is always ready to help and to forgive.

If we could improve our understanding of the Father, grasp His divinity, and embrace His compassion, we would be a lot more inclined to embrace that divinity and deserve that compassion. Every one of us will have occasion to utter "the voice of [our] supplications" in prayer, and sometimes that will be earnest, anguished, painful prayer. The promise of the scriptures and the eloquence of the psalms is that God is "good, and ready to forgive."

We can lift up our soul unto Him for the glorious reception that soul will receive, knowing with absolute certainty that He "will not always chide" but that His mercy is "from everlasting to everlasting."

PSALM 89:9

*Thou rulest the raging of the sea: when the waves thereof
arise, thou stillest them.*

There are times in all of our lives when storms of emotion, tribulation, or sorrow swirl about us and we plead for someone to still those storms. Speaking of the military advantage of a great navy, the Roman orator Cicero is reported to have said, "He that rules the waves rules the world." Little did he know how true that was. God rules the waves and He does rule the world. One of the greatest of all the stories of the New Testament is the power demonstrated by the Savior in just such a circumstance.

After having taught for many hours, Jesus invited His disciples to cross over to the other side of the Galilee. As is so often the case in the Holy Land, a great storm arose while they were crossing this sea that they knew so well, and "the waves beat into the ship, so that it was now full."[161]

Consider that men like Peter, James, and John were with Jesus on that ship, men who made their living on that sea, who knew its every current and all aspects of its personality. It makes us realize how serious the storm must have been to frighten *them* so much that they awakened the Savior, saying, "Master, carest thou not that we perish?"[162]

It is tender to me that Jesus was asleep through all of this, which speaks of at least two things: first of all, His peace of mind in any storm, and second, the incredible fatigue that He must have felt in giving so much to His ministry and the multitudes. In any case, He was awakened as a result of His disciples' fear. He answered their faith by arising and rebuking the wind, saying to the elements, "Peace, be still. And the wind ceased, and there was a great calm."[163]

But after rebuking the wind, He at least mildly rebuked His beloved disciples, for He turned to them and said, "Why are ye so fearful? how is it that ye have no faith?" Their reaction? "And they feared exceedingly, and said one to another, What manner of man is this, that even the wind and the sea obey him?"[164]

From time to time we all have occasion to cry out, "Master, the Tempest Is Raging"—times when we "bow in . . . grief" and "torrents of . . . anguish sweep o'er [our] sinking soul." But if we are in the company of the Savior of the world, "the Master of ocean and earth and skies," He will calm the winds and still the waves.[165] Truly we can all be less fearful. Surely with God's help we will have more faith.

PSALM 89:30–34

If his children forsake my law, and walk not in my judgments;

If they break my statutes, and keep not my commandments;

Then will I visit their transgression with the rod, and their iniquity with stripes.

Nevertheless my lovingkindness will I not utterly take from him, nor suffer my faithfulness to fail.

My covenant will I not break, nor alter the thing that is gone out of my lips.

We would be foolish to believe that breaking the commandments does not take a toll upon us. The very purpose of a commandment is to mark a path that, if we follow it, will spare us personal pain and unneeded sorrow. In breaking a commandment there is (as in Newtonian physics) a reaction to every such action. That reaction will always have some kind of negative result.

But God will never remove His lovingkindness from us, nor will He suffer His faithfulness to fail unless our own actions insist on it. We can be assured that He will not break His covenants with us nor alter any of the words that have been spoken in our behalf. The scriptures are replete with the declaration that "what I the Lord have spoken, I have spoken, and I excuse not myself; and though the heavens and the earth shall pass away, my word shall not pass away, but shall all be fulfilled."[166]

Those words, those promises and expressions all speak to His love, His goodness, His fatherhood. So the sooner we can see His laws and statutes—His commandments—as being for our good, the better. Furthermore, it is encouraging to know there is virtually nothing we can do that would ever put us permanently beyond the reach of His mercy and His redemption. His kindness will not be taken from us. His faithfulness will not fail. He will not break His promises, and He has promised to stand by us forever and, if we wish it, to redeem our souls from sin.

Trust in all the things God has spoken. Know that if you want to have His grace, you can. God always keeps His covenants with us. We can find great joy in life if we will keep our covenants with Him.

PSALM 89:33–34

Nevertheless my lovingkindness will I not utterly take from him, nor suffer my faithfulness to fail.

My covenant will I not break, nor alter the thing that is gone out of my lips.

PSALMS 94:9–10; 100:3, 5; 119:99–100

He that planted the ear, shall he not hear? he that formed the eye, shall he not see?

He that chastiseth the heathen, shall not he correct? he that teacheth man knowledge, shall not he know?

———

Know ye that the Lord he is God: it is he that hath made us, and not we ourselves; we are his people, and the sheep of his pasture. . . .

And his truth endureth to all generations.

———

I have more understanding than all my teachers: for thy testimonies are my meditation.

I understand more than the ancients, because I keep thy precepts.

These passages are a gentle rebuke to those who may be tempted to consider themselves so bright they are smarter than God.

Perhaps the only serious risk I have seen in the world of academic accomplishment is the pride and vanity that can come with it, the arrogance of a few who say not to the hand or to the foot but to God Himself, "I have no need of thee."[167] The vanity of a brilliant person is a tragedy indeed if in any way that gift takes the recipient of it away from the God who gave it in the first place. "To be learned is good if they hearken unto the counsels of God" is almost the only caution one truly needs in the marvelous pursuit of knowledge.[168] If one hears philosophical or scientific truth, did not "He that planted the ear" also hear—and indeed declare—those truths initially? If one sees the beauty of great art or literature, did not "he that formed the eye" also first see it and share it with the artist or the writer? Can we not find in ourselves the humility to acknowledge that *some* ear might be greater than ours, that *some* eye might be more perceptive than the one we possess? Could not a learned man or woman grant that He who has taught us everything and is the receptacle of all knowledge knows the things that we know and some other truths besides? Some of those additional truths include matters of faith and devotion that will save our souls in eternity.

Everyone needs to guard against vanity and arrogance, but especially bright, talented people need to be careful because, truth be told, they have the most to be vain and arrogant about. History would suggest that keeping up such a guard isn't easy—our vanity is forever at odds with our humility and frequently triumphs in that battle.

The fact of the matter is, the more capable we are, the more humble we should be. God "is God: it is he that hath made us." We should bow our head and bend our knee at His grandeur, at least in part because He has bestowed some part of it on us.

PSALM 105:15

Touch not mine anointed, and do my prophets no harm.

David himself gave us a most indelible lesson in this matter when he refused to take the life of Saul, his anointed but adversarial king. It did not matter that Saul sought David's life repeatedly and would have killed him if he could. The reverse was not to be. David honored the office, and in so doing honored the man who held it. Indeed, he was distraught when others were not as respectful of their king as he and lamented grievously the day Saul's life was taken by another.

We have anointed prophets, apostles, and leaders in our day. They have never claimed to be perfect, as indeed only one human being in all of history has been. But imperfect as they are, they represent the One who *was* perfect—a staggering responsibility indeed. Trying to be the best they can be, these leaders have been called to perform certain functions and carry out certain duties in the name of God. No one is more conscious of that responsibility than these priesthood bearers themselves. No one feels the weight of it more, no one is more mindful of his limitations, no one worries more that however good he is, he needs to be even better. We who observe them know this and love them for their service. We see so few limitations. And while we strive to sustain them, to join in holding them up in their service, we also can at the very least not harm them, not detract or decry or destroy them in word or in deed.

President Boyd K. Packer has often quoted this account from the life of the much-criticized Abraham Lincoln as told by one of his biographers. Facing a delegation of adversaries critical of how he was waging the Civil War, Lincoln said:

"Gentlemen, suppose all the property you possessed were in gold, and you had placed it in the hands of a [man] to carry across the Niagara River on a rope. With slow, cautious steps he walks to the rope, bearing your all. Would you shake the cable and keep shouting at him, ' . . . Stand up a little straighter; . . . stoop a little more; go a little faster; lean more to the south; now lean a little more to the north?' Would that be your behavior in such an emergency?

"No, you would hold your breath, every one of you, as well as your tongues. You would keep your hands off until he was safe on the other side."[169]

In the much higher and more important world of spiritual service, we need to pray for and sustain our leaders. They are wonderfully good men and women, doing the best they can to know God's will for the Church and to honor that will. And they have "an unction from the Holy One," which adds sanctity to their honest efforts.[170] We owe our loyalty to them in no small part out of devotion to that Holy One whose work they are called to do.

PSALM 113:9

He maketh the barren woman to keep house, and to be a joyful mother of children. Praise ye the Lord.

One of the deep and poignant sorrows we often find among members of the Church is the pain that a worthy woman feels in not being married or that an equally worthy married woman feels when she is unable to bear children. The spirit of this psalm has brought great peace to many, reminding us that the prophets have promised that God will not withhold any righteous blessing from the righteous women who will continue to walk by faith, continue to be true, continue to live with hope.

The promise to every worthy woman is that she will have a chance to marry in time or in eternity, and an equal promise to every worthy woman is that she will have an opportunity to "keep house, and to be a joyful mother of children" somewhere, sometime, someday.

We do not know all the particulars of how that is done or under what circumstances the miracle of that promise will unfold, but it will unfold. This promise is meant to be a great assurance to those who have worthy desires of marriage and children and family life with their eternal bonds of love.

Those desires will be realized. God has promised it. And it will be a joyful experience.

PSALM 116:15

Precious in the sight of the Lord is the death of his saints.

Funerals are among the most sacred and spiritual meetings held in The Church of Jesus Christ of Latter-day Saints. On occasion those deaths can seem untimely—an infant, a young child, a teenager, a missionary, a young parent leaving an even younger family, and so forth. But even when lives have been lived long and fully, there is still a genuine loss at having them pass. This might be a spouse, a parent, or a grandparent, or it might simply be a friend or neighbor. On those occasions when we memorialize their lives and praise their names, it is appropriate, as the scriptures say, to "weep for the loss of them that die."[171]

Tears at the passing of good people are the price we pay for love in this world. We realize how precious these people are to us and how precious their lives have been, so it is very easy to see why they are indeed "precious in the sight of the Lord." In that sense, even as we feel such loss in our lives, how joyful it must be for that person, other loved ones, and the Lord Himself to have such a joyful reunion beyond the veil. Nothing is more "precious" than a humble, worthy, loving life. How grateful we should be, then, when the Lord will say to such an one, "Well done, thou good and faithful servant: . . . enter thou into the joy of thy lord."[172] It is worth letting them go in order for them to behold that face and hear those words.

PSALM 118:6

*The Lord is on my side; I will not fear: what can man do
unto me?*

We sing in the Church, "Who's on the Lord's side? Who? Now is the time to show. We ask it fearlessly: Who's on the Lord's side? Who?"[173]

Surely in the battles of life and the vicissitudes we face there is nothing that could be more reassuring than to know that we are on the Lord's side and that, in turn, He is on ours. This does not mean the battles will cease. It does not mean the travail will be short-lived or instantly overcome. But it does mean that we can fight with confidence against woes and oppositions that eventually will yield to divine influence.

Of course it is particularly painful if these woes and oppositions come from another person. Life is hard enough when it is just life, but it is very distressing when problems arise because of a fellow human being. But so it has been since Cain turned upon Abel. Men and women regularly hurt other men and women. All we can do—and it is enough—is be true to our principles even if others abandon theirs. To those who keep His commandments, God is a permanent ally.

Stephen was one of the early martyrs in the cause of Christ, but he was on the Lord's side and he did not fear. His devotion cost him his life, but he did not die afraid. There was, in a very real sense, literally nothing that man could do to him that mattered. Stephen "being full of the Holy Ghost, looked up stedfastly into heaven, and saw the glory of God, and Jesus standing on the right hand of God." His last words were those "calling upon God, and saying, Lord Jesus, receive my spirit. And he kneeled down, and cried with a loud voice, Lord, lay not this sin to their charge. And when he had said this, he fell asleep."[174] What a thrilling description of peaceful confidence when we are on the Lord's side and He is on ours.

> *Our ensign to the world*
> *Is floating proudly now.*
> *No coward bears our flag;*
> *Who's on the Lord's side? Who?*[175]

In the eternal battle between good and evil, there is nothing others can do that will hurt us permanently or harm us eternally if we know we are on the Lord's side and He is on ours.

PSALM 118:24

This is the day which the Lord hath made; we will rejoice and be glad in it.

One of the great temptations of life is to spend so much time looking back or so much time looking ahead that we fail to see the opportunity right in front of us. Certainly we should study the past. We all ought to learn the lessons of history. Many of our scriptures have been given to teach us about challenges that others have faced in the past so we can avoid those dangers when they come to us. Furthermore, we all ought to plan for the future. We all ought to look ahead. None of us should be surprised when tomorrow comes and new circumstances present themselves. But having learned from the past and while preparing for the future, we can in reality only deal with the present day. Life has to be lived in the present tense. The current hour is the only one we have.

It is telling that when the fearful Moses was to rescue the enslaved Israelites, he said to the Lord, "Behold, when I come unto the children of Israel, and shall say unto them, The God of your fathers hath sent me unto you; and they shall say to me, What is his name? what shall I say unto them?" God replied to His prophet, "I AM THAT I

AM: . . . Thus shalt thou say unto the children of Israel, I AM hath sent me unto you."[176] Grammatically (and theologically) speaking, that is a divine declaration of God in the present tense. (He had just said to Moses, "*I am* the God of thy father, the God of Abraham, the God of Isaac, and the God of Jacob."[177]) Yes, He has been with us in the past and yes, He will be with us in the future. He is Alpha and Omega, the First and the Last, the Beginning and the End. These are all titles applicable to the Lord. But when we need Him urgently, when we need Him in great faith, when challenges are immediate and overwhelming, He is with us in the present tense.

I AM, I AM, I AM. Surely God is trying to teach us a great truth here. He is. He does live. He does act in our lives. He is engaged with us in the first-person, present-tense, active voice. Nothing could be more comforting.

PSALM 119:19

*I am a stranger in the earth: hide not thy commandments
from me.*

One of the realizations we come to regularly in our lives is that
this world we live in now is not our home. It's a wonderful
place. It's a beautiful place. It's God's creation. And it is part of His
plan for our salvation. But it is not our home. We had a veil drawn
across our minds before we came here, and we have the promise that
after this life is over, we will return to that place that really is our
home. We will both remember what we knew before we came into
mortality and take with us many wonderful lessons that we learned
while here. Nevertheless, while we are here in a telestial world, it can
sometimes be a lonely place. We can feel like strangers here.

Jacob, born to Lehi and Sariah in the wilderness of their affliction, had a difficult life by any standard and felt something of this
loneliness of which we speak. Near the end of his life, he said, "The
time passed away with us, and also our lives passed away like as it were
unto us a dream, we being a lonesome and a solemn people, wander-
ers, cast out from Jerusalem, born in tribulation, in a wilderness, and

hated of our brethren, which caused wars and contentions; wherefore, we did mourn out our days."[178]

Obviously not all of our days are spent in mourning and not all of our days are lonely. Indeed we pray that there will always be bright days and wonderful fellowship among the Saints of God and within the household of faith. But, still, this world is not our home and we are not to live as if we were going to stay here. Thus the commandments of God. Little wonder that the Psalmist cries, "Hide not thy commandments from me." Obeying them is the only way we can make it through this sometimes hostile world.

PSALM 119:59–60

I thought on my ways, and turned my feet unto thy testimonies.

I made haste, and delayed not to keep thy commandments.

In the parable of the prodigal son, perhaps the most telling phrase is that after he had made his mistakes, gone his way, and squandered his fortune, the young man "came to himself."[179] Every one of us needs to "come to ourselves." We need to "think on our ways" and correct these ways in the process. Like the prodigal son, we need to "[turn our] feet unto [our] testimonies." We need to make haste to come back—to come back to our Father, to come back to our family, to come back to our future, to come back to our faith.

In a similar vein, Lehi's plea to his wayward sons may well apply to all of us: "Awake, my sons; put on the armor of righteousness. Shake off the chains with which ye are bound, and come forth out of obscurity, and arise from the dust."[180] We need to wake up to the consequences of our actions and recognize where we may be going wrong.

It is interesting that one of Satan's greatest ploys is to keep us from "thinking on our ways." He wants to keep us busy with games or hobbies or preoccupations or worries or economics. There are plenty of things to occupy our minds and divert our thoughts, but some portion of our day (and indeed this may lead to the salvation of our whole life) ought to be devoted to "thinking on our ways."

Then, with haste and conviction, we should turn our feet toward God. He is loving. He is waiting for us. His arms are extended. But He will not force or turn our feet. We must do that. Chances are we will never feel inclined to do so unless we think upon our ways in some period of self-examination and self-assessment. Don't delay. Make haste.

PSALM 119:67, 71–72

Before I was afflicted I went astray: but now have I kept thy word. . . .

It is good for me that I have been afflicted; that I might learn thy statutes.

The law of thy mouth is better unto me than thousands of gold and silver.

We would not like to think that we have to be afflicted in order to learn the lessons of life, but sometimes we do. Alma made a great appeal to the Zoramites who had been afflicted with great poverty and had become socially despised. Ironically but not surprisingly, this had a valuable effect upon them because they turned to hear the word of the Lord. In that regard Alma said, "I behold that ye are lowly in heart. . . . Because ye are compelled to be humble blessed are ye; for a man sometimes, if he is compelled to be humble, seeketh repentance; . . . [and] shall find mercy; and he that findeth mercy and endureth to the end the same shall be saved."[181]

And then this prophetic insight: "Because ye were compelled to be humble ye were blessed, [but] do ye not suppose that they are more blessed who truly humble themselves because of the word? . . . Therefore, blessed are they who humble themselves *without* being compelled to be humble."[182]

We do learn from our mistakes. Certainly we should. We are foolish beyond measure if we don't. Many can say with the Psalmist that until they were afflicted, they were going astray. In such circumstances perhaps only our affliction brings us back to our senses, brings us back to keeping His word. With that perspective we all should be able to say, even with hard lessons and difficult experiences, "It is good for me that I have been afflicted."

PSALM 119:94

I am thine, save me; for I have sought thy precepts.

This is one of the shortest lines in this little collection of thoughts, but it is one of the sweetest. Whatever our difficulty, whatever our trials, whatever our problems, we go forward on the reassurance of one grand principle, one fundamental element of our faith—that we are God's children, that He wants very much to bless us, and that He does this ultimately through the gift of His Only Begotten Son.

The Savior once said (as quoted by Isaiah) that, as unlikely as it is, a mother could forget the child to whom she had given birth and whom she had nursed and loved. Knowing a mother's love makes that most improbable, nearly impossible, to imagine—but it would be more imaginable than that either the Father or the Son would ever forget us. The reason they would not (could not?) forget us is because with the approbation of the Father, the Son has "graven [us] upon the palms of [His] hands."[183] In our extremity, we can always make claim upon those wounds—those scarred reminders that a great price has been paid for our salvation. Having paid such a price, neither the Father nor the Son is going to give up on us now. Following their precepts will save us.

PSALMS 119:103, 105; 12:6; 18:28

How sweet are thy words unto my taste! yea, sweeter than honey to my mouth! . . .

Thy word is a lamp unto my feet, and a light unto my path.

The words of the Lord are pure words: as silver tried in a furnace of earth, purified seven times.

For thou wilt light my candle: the Lord my God will enlighten my darkness.

The scriptures—the words of the Lord—as they came anciently and in modern times are the most secure means we have for knowing who God is, what His purposes are, and what He expects from His children in mortality. The scriptures are our standards for measuring truth—our "standard works." Without them we "would have dwindled in unbelief," not understanding God's mysteries and not having His commandments "always before our eyes."[184]

One wonders if God will hold us guiltless if we treat lightly the words He has spoken and the lives given for those words?[185] One by one, the great figures of the Old Testament gave their lives that we might have that great record. He sent His Only Begotten into the world, and His life was sacrificed (along with the lives of His Apostles) in order that we might have the teachings of the New Testament. Many of the prophets of God whose words are recorded in the Book of Mormon laid down their lives and sealed their testimonies with their blood in order that those in our day might know of His dealings—and of Christ's appearance—in the New World. The Lord sent the Prophet Joseph Smith, who likewise sealed his testimony with his own blood, that we might have the truths contained in modern revelation. Joseph's brother Hyrum gave his life at the same time. Others have done so since.

It seems highly unlikely that after the Lord has done all this for us, has given to this world the best lives and the best blood in it in order to record and preserve His holy word, that He will be pleased with careless—or no—attention to those revelations. The "silver" of the scriptures has been refined in a furnace, all right, in part because those prophets and apostles went into a personal furnace to provide them.

The word of God is an iron rod to lead us through mists of darkness, a feast of divine sustenance in an otherwise fallen world. No lamp could be more reliable in the dark of the night and no sweeter taste could come to the lips of a people when there is a famine in the land—"not a famine of bread, nor a thirst for water, but of hearing the words of the Lord."[186]

Thank heaven and all eternity for the scriptures, "for behold, the words of Christ will tell you all things what ye should do."[187] And as with the prophet Lehi, so too with each of us. "As he read [the words of the book], he was filled with the Spirit of the Lord."[188] Such precious, piercing experience with the Godhead through the medium of the revealed word makes that experience sweeter than honey to our mouths. The first foundation stones of my testimony came from my youthful experience reading the scriptures. They sustained me then and they sustain me now. We ought to be so grateful that the heavens are open, that God "speaks," not just "spake," because in times of trouble and always we need "a lamp unto [our] feet, and a light unto [our] path."

PSALM 119:108

Accept, I beseech thee, the freewill offerings of my mouth, O Lord, and teach me thy judgments.

Sometimes we are forced to say the right things, as if righteousness could be coerced. In a court of law, for instance, we are under oath to "tell the truth, the whole truth, and nothing but the truth." Early in our lives our parents told us to tell the truth, or to apologize for a misdeed, or to say "I'm sorry." Required expressions have their place, but how much more wonderful when, of our own volition, we offer to the Lord and others "the freewill offerings of [our] mouth." These might include—but are not limited to—words of love, words of kindness, words of patience, words of compassion.

We make a freewill offering of our mouth every time we offer a prayer that is honest and from the heart. We make a freewill offering of our mouth every time we bear a testimony or teach a truth. Furthermore, we can give such expressions even more freely and generously than we do. We can tell those near and dear to us that we love them, that they mean everything to us, and that life would not be as sweet or sacred without their companionship. We can speak courteously to the stranger in the store and the fellow driving the car in the other lane of traffic. We can open our mouths in taking the gospel to those who know nothing of what we believe or what we teach.

In sacred places we speak sacred words, and we sometimes do that kneeling at an altar. How wonderful to contemplate that such truth would never have to be forced from our lips, that love would never have to be extracted from us, that forgiveness would never be granted by us only because we "had to." Freewill offerings come from the heart. That is where our words should come from—quickly and generously and often. They ought to reflect our devotion to God—freely.

PSALM 119:108

Accept, I beseech thee, the freewill offerings of my mouth, O Lord, and teach me thy judgments.

PSALM 127:1

Except the Lord build the house, they labour in vain that build it: except the Lord keep the city, the watchman waketh but in vain.

Surely one of the lessons we learn in our walk of life is that without the Lord's help, we cannot succeed in any significant way. This psalm speaks of building a house, but it might as well speak of building a family or a profession, a government or a philosophy of life. In these endeavors—as noble as the intent might be and as laborious as the effort is—none of it will succeed in the end without the Lord's help, without the Lord's sanction, without the Lord's protection, without the Lord's approval. We can't build an institution of any consequence without His help and we cannot defend that institution without it, either.

Perhaps the best short poem ever written by Percy Bysshe Shelley is a haunting piece entitled "Ozymandias." It is a sonnet composed in response to an inscription chiseled onto the base of a collapsed and broken statue from the period of the great Rameses II of Egypt, which read, "King of Kings am I, Osymandias. If anyone would know how great I am and where I lie, let him surpass one of my works." The grand irony, of course, is that the king and his art—to say nothing of his fame and his empire—now lie in a heap for all to see exactly "where I lie." Shelley's poem is as follows:

> *I met a traveller from an antique land*
> *Who said: Two vast and trunkless legs of stone*
> *Stand in the desert . . . Near them, on the sand,*
> *Half sunk, a shattered visage lies, whose frown,*
> *And wrinkled lip, and sneer of cold command,*
> *Tell that its sculptor well those passions read*
> *Which yet survive, stamped on these lifeless things,*
> *The hand that mocked them, and the heart that fed:*
> *And on the pedestal these words appear:*
> *"My name is Ozymandias, king of kings:*
> *Look on my works, ye Mighty, and despair!"*
> *Nothing beside remains. Round the decay*
> *Of that colossal wreck, boundless and bare,*
> *The lone and level sands stretch far away.*[189]

Except the Lord build us and the structures of our lives, we labor in vain to build them at all.

PSALM 127:3–5

Lo, children are an heritage of the Lord: and the fruit of the womb is his reward.

As arrows are in the hand of a mighty man; so are children of the youth.

Happy is the man that hath his quiver full of them: they shall not be ashamed, but they shall speak with the enemies in the gate.

Sooner or later every one of us comes to realize that of all the human relationships in life, and indeed in all the temporal pursuits undertaken in a mortal world, nothing is as rewarding as life with and the love of our family. Children truly are "an heritage of the Lord." Most parents feel great joy in their children most of the time. But when circumstances go awry, children can also be the source of their parents' greatest pain.

We teach that God is our Father and that we are His offspring, His spiritual children. This eternal perspective on and affection for the concept of family adds to the significance of our earthly relationships. God wants to bless us as we want to bless our children.

He weeps and worries about us, as we weep and worry about our children. Truly we get an education in being more godlike when we bring children into the world and see them as the "heritage of the Lord" that they are.

Sometimes in mortal life, with its various physical limitations and emotional challenges, families are not always calm and contented. But with the eternal understanding the gospel gives, we know they can and eventually will be. Trust God when children wander. They are still yours and they are still His. They are "an heritage of the Lord."

Happiness at home is truly the greatest happiness of all. Keep giving your love to your children—just the way God keeps giving His love to you. Happy will be the man and woman who hath a "quiver full" of such arrows—even if they weren't always straight arrows and no matter how challenging they might have been in their growing-up years!

PSALM 133:1

*Behold, how good and how pleasant it is for brethren to
dwell together in unity!*

Our bodies, our souls, and our psyches were meant to be at peace.
We all know the illness of the physical body when some element of our health is out of order, when some process is not in unity
with all of the others. It is even more wrenching when that happens
in the mind or in the spirit.

For example, real illness can come from the guilt that accompanies going against the unity of our beliefs, against the integrity of our
moral commitments. We have all seen examples where there has been
a lack of unity in a marriage, or in a family, or in an athletic team, or
in the community at large.

Paul taught that a body—whether that body be of an individual
person or a church or a nation—cannot war against itself, cannot be
antagonistic one part to another, cannot survive with one element
saying that it has no need of the other.[190] Life is happier at every level
if we are unified and harmonious, always allowing for differences
of opinion and individual personalities, but never letting legitimate

distinctions and uniqueness bring pain or strife so serious that it compromises the health of the person.

God expects us to be unified as His children and as His Church. He expects us to "dwell together in unity."

Indeed, one of the great characteristics of the latter-day Zion is that the people will be "of one heart and one mind, and [dwell together] in righteousness."[191] In His magnificent Intercessory Prayer, Christ pled for that unity in the lives of His disciples.[192] Later the New Testament Saints did believe and "were of one heart and of one soul."[193]

We are, as members of the Church, the body of Christ. He expects unity of purpose and sublimation of selfishness when the health of the whole body is at stake. This helps the entire enterprise—as well as the individuals in it—to fend off difficult times or triumph over them when they come. Truly if we are not one in the family of God, we are not His.[194]

PSALM 139:23

Search me, O God, and know my heart: try me, and know my thoughts.

Within The Church of Jesus Christ of Latter-day Saints, there is a long tradition of interviews. We are regularly invited to go before our leaders (and they to go before theirs) to see if we are worthy for this assignment or that privilege. In our childhood, this might involve preparation for baptism or confirmation. As teenagers, this experience might come with an Aaronic Priesthood ordination or a Young Women achievement program. This moment of self-examination gets more serious as the years go by and the complexities of gospel living unfold. As temptations become greater, interviews get more rigorous—in preparation for missions, for temple experiences, and for other sacred moments in life. By the time we have lived a full measure in the Church, we will have had many chances to be interviewed regarding our standing before the Lord.

But far more important and far more personal than the interviews we have with Church leaders is the interview—daily, hourly, moment by moment—that we should have before the Lord. We know from the scriptures that He sees all, that "all things are present before

[His] eyes," and that He is always in our midst.[195] How crucial, then, that in every waking hour of our lives and every moment of our discipleship we say with honesty, "Search me, O God, and know my heart: try me, and know my thoughts." That is an interview the Lord is constantly giving us (whether we agree to it or not). He is searching our hearts, and He surely knows our thoughts. We would do well to be worthy of such examination "at all times and in all things, and in all places."[196]

PSALM 141:3

Set a watch, O Lord, before my mouth; keep the door of my
lips.

We have noted earlier in this book that there is power in speech and great influence in words. But there are some times when we ought *not* to speak, times when quite literally we ought to keep our mouths shut. Part of the difference between the Old Testament and the New was that in the Old Testament there was a more pronounced theory of retribution. The reasoning was that if you say something ill of me, I can say something just as ill of you in return. And so it went for hundreds of years, "an eye for an eye, and a tooth for a tooth."[197]

One of the greatest things ever said about the Savior was the testimony of His chief Apostle Peter, who recorded that "when he was reviled, [he] reviled not."[198] Gospel virtues like patience, long-suffering, kindness, and charity all suggest that we not do harm, spoken or otherwise, even when such harm has been done to us. Some things we simply endure. A certain part of a Christian's life is to "suffer in silence" rather than to add to the trouble, add to the pain, add to the mistake. Two wrongs don't make a right; if someone has wronged us, we gain nothing by replying in kind.

Perhaps nowhere is that lesson more readily taught and more readily needed than in the daily life of a home and family. There are some things that a spouse should never say to a mate, even when provoked. There are some things a parent should never say to a child, even when patience has been tried to its very limit. There are certainly some things that a child should never say to a parent if he or she is to keep the great fifth commandment given by God.

We should learn to curb our tongues. We should remember that spoken words can never be recalled and may be remembered in sorrow and regret forever. Not everything we feel has to be said. Almost nothing we think in anger has to be said. Truly our world would be a happier and better place if in times of distress and trouble we could cry out, "Set a watch, O Lord, before my mouth; keep the door of my lips."

PSALM 141:5

Let the righteous smite me; it shall be a kindness: and let him reprove me; it shall be an excellent oil, which shall not break my head: for yet my prayer also shall be in their calamities.

It truly takes a magnanimous soul to invite correction, to welcome constructive criticism, to be humbled by the counsel of the Lord and His servants. It may be a little strong to think of the righteous "smiting" anyone, but the point is that if a comment is made righteously, it indeed should be and ultimately would be "a kindness" if it resulted in an improved life. In the same spirit, if reproof is necessary, reproof is "an excellent oil." We think of the use of consecrated oil being administered to the head of a loved one in a time of need. Surely that oil does not "break [our] head." It is rather a gentle, even soothing, application.

It would be an advantage in our lives if we could be humble enough to accept any useful counsel as a kindness, and any caution, even a call to repentance, as "excellent oil." Through it all, even in extreme moments that may seem to us like "calamities," we should let our prayer of gratitude ascend for our own growth and for the concern of those who love us enough to correct us.

PSALM 144:12

That our sons may be as plants grown up in their youth; that our daughters may be as corner stones, polished after the similitude of a palace.

This phrase from the Psalmist is one of the loveliest scriptural images we have regarding children. We all want our children to be the best they can be, and we want them to be better than we were. Every parent hopes that his or her children will be safe and pure, strong and righteous. It would be an unusual parent indeed who would not wish a child to be good, to be honest, to be a responsible, contributing citizen in a family, a church, and a nation.

Much in the Hebraic tradition of the scriptures deals with sons and priesthood principles. Yet so often we fail to recognize how many stunningly beautiful things are said about women—our mothers and daughters and sisters. What could be more inspiring than to think of our daughters as the corner stones of a palace, even corner stones of the temple—like unto Christ, who is "the chief corner stone" of the Church and of our lives.[199]

God has no favorites. He does not love His sons more than He loves His daughters, and truly His daughters often—very often—set an example and a standard for His sons that the latter dearly need. Women have proven to be the salvation of many a man, and in our lives they truly are foundational gems—rock-solid jewels of faith and fidelity that make our individual lives, our homes, our churches, and our communities polished and more pure. They are "after the similitude of a palace," and we thank heaven for the godliness in them.

PSALMS 145:14; 146:8

The Lord upholdeth all that fall, and raiseth up all those that be bowed down.

The Lord openeth the eyes of the blind: the Lord raiseth them that are bowed down: the Lord loveth the righteous.

As a concluding thought in this eclectic and very personal selection from the psalms, perhaps nothing could be more fitting "for times of trouble" than this last promise. We began with the assertion that God is for us. We end with the reassurance that He can and wants to and will raise "all those that be bowed down"—and all of us are bowed down sometime. If we are bowed down with worry or sorrow or tribulation, we can be lifted up. If we are spiritually blind, or spiritually deaf, or spiritually lame, or even spiritually dead, God can heal all those imperfections and restore us to strength and solid standing. If any one of us falls, we can be raised from it.

Nothing is more certain in the scriptures (and in the psalms) than that God will not falter or fail us, that He sleeps not neither does He slumber, that when we are weary and can run no longer He will lift us on the wings of eagles. The intent of this book is to show that divine love for us, to show God's light shining in the dark places of our lives. But such an outreach to those in darkness or difficulty would not be complete (or even responsible) if it did not conclude with the understanding that we should never *choose* darkness, we should never wallow in despair, we should never make a habit of courting trouble or looking for it if we haven't had any recently.

The Father, Son, and Holy Ghost are indeed there to "[uphold] all that fall," but we should never keep falling intentionally, nor should we just lie there—again—waiting for the grace of God to pick up the pieces—again. In short, through all our trials in life we must truly strive to be righteous. We may not ever be free from pain. We certainly won't be free from problems. We won't always have bright, sunny days. Sometimes money, talent, opportunity, and tempers will be short. These psalms have reminded us that much of the time there will be trouble enough to go around, with headaches and heartaches in every direction.

But through all this we can be righteous! While we are waiting for help, we can try to help ourselves. While we are struggling with a problem, we can look for the chance to relieve another who faces an even greater challenge than our own. We know we can't escape trouble, but we should do everything humanly possible to escape sin. Heaven deserves at least that much from us in gratitude for our being raised up when we are bowed down, for being upheld when we fall. "The Lord loveth the righteous," and no amount of difficulty in life should keep us from qualifying for that designation.

SECTION 2
THE MESSIAH

SOME MESSIANIC PSALMS

Perhaps the reason Jesus quoted Psalms more than any other book of the Old Testament is because He found His teachings, His mission, and His majesty recorded there in such a pronounced way. As such, surely He was using this favored book as preeminent among all the earlier texts that were witnesses of His divinity. In a sense all of the Old Testament, like the law of Moses found there, was something of a "schoolmaster to bring us unto Christ," as the Apostle Paul said.[200] But whatever elementary teachings other parts of the ancient records give us about the Messiah—and some obviously give more than others—the psalms give us the most. In terms of Paul's metaphor, these lyrical declarations seem to take us directly to graduate school regarding the merciful nature and compassion of the Savior of the world.

While it is not quite literally so, the reader can have the impression that almost all of these 150 "chapters" have some reference to, some application about, or some meaning found in the life and mission of the Son of God. When the resurrected Jesus joined His two brethren on the road to Emmaus, Luke says He began "at Moses and all the prophets," and "expounded unto them in all the scriptures the things concerning himself."[201] From His own lips we know the psalms were among the principal texts to which He referred in this setting because He used them in other settings. Appearing to the Apostles just prior to His ascension into heaven, Jesus "said unto them, These are the words which I spake unto you, while I was yet with you, that all things must be fulfilled, which were written in the law of Moses, and in the prophets, *and in the psalms,* concerning me. Then opened he their understanding, that they might understand the scriptures."[202]

Perhaps noting just a few of the more obvious Messianic psalms will be enough to invite the reader's consideration of many others, finding in unexpected places a reference or an analogy or a type that takes one once again to the life, mission, and message of Jesus Christ.

PSALM 2

Why do the heathen rage, and the people imagine a vain thing?

The kings of the earth set themselves, and the rulers take counsel together, against the Lord, and against his anointed, . . .

Yet have I set my king upon my holy hill of Zion.

I will declare the decree: the Lord hath said unto me, Thou art my Son; this day have I begotten thee. . . .

Be wise now therefore, O ye kings: be instructed, ye judges of the earth.

Serve the Lord with fear, and rejoice with trembling.

Kiss the Son, lest he be angry, and ye perish from the way, when his wrath is kindled but a little. Blessed are all they that put their trust in him.

This is the first of the many Messianic psalms included in the Old Testament collection. Linked with Psalm 1, which was discussed earlier in this book, Psalm 2 has generally been considered an introduction to the psalms that follow.[203] Of course, it is significant that any introduction to these supplications would also introduce the idea of the Messiah, inasmuch as so many of the psalms touch on that theme.

In terms of the troubles we face in life—the theme of this book— it should be noted that the first line of this psalm poses trouble for God and His Son. The heathen (and they could be defined as every-one who does not have faith) "rage" and the people (a term broad enough to include almost everyone) "imagine a vain thing." Yes, early in the psalms we are to learn that we are not the only ones who have troubles, but that members of the Godhead and the angels who as-sist them have troubles of their own—us! Everything in the universe seems to obey the divine order of things but us—God's children, the family born of Him spiritually and destined to become like Him in eternity if we will but resist raging against His plan and imagining vain things that divert us.

Note that *vain* has at least two meanings in the scriptures and both are applicable here—"vain" meaning self-centered, conceited, and excessively proud, and "vain" meaning without effect, futile, without success. Both meanings are applicable to "the heathen" and "the people" who do not embrace the gospel of Jesus Christ, who "take counsel together, against the Lord [the Father], and against his anointed [the Son]." As Christ moved toward Gethsemane and Calvary, His enemies—the kings and rulers of His day, as it were— "took counsel how they might entangle him in his talk,"[204] "took counsel against Jesus to put him to death,"[205] and in the end "took counsel, and bought with [Judas's blood money] the potter's field, to bury strangers in."[206] How "vain"—conceited and futile—such rebel-lion was in attempting to withstand the salvation of the Almighty. Knowing all of this would happen, yet God the Father of us all set the King of us all, His Only Begotten Son, on the throne in Zion and declared to all the world His divinity. "Thou art my Son, this day have I begotten thee." So the Apostle Paul would quote to the rulers of the synagogue at Antioch in declaring that this "Son" was Jesus Christ, not David, as many of the Israelites believed and taught.[207]

These are simple, straightforward declarations of the truth. This is the way it is. We might rage and insist it be otherwise, but it is not. God has a plan for our exaltation, and His Only Begotten Son is central to it. So rather than rebellion and vanity, raging and conceit, the call is for wisdom and humility, for understanding and obedience. "Be wise now therefore, O ye kings: be instructed, ye judges of the earth. Serve the Lord with fear, and rejoice with trembling. Kiss the Son [out of loyalty, as one kisses the emblem of a king]. . . . Blessed are all they that put their trust in him."

PSALM 8

O Lord our Lord, how excellent is thy name in all the earth! who hast set thy glory above the heavens.

Out of the mouth of babes and sucklings hast thou ordained strength because of thine enemies, that thou mightest still the enemy and the avenger.

When I consider thy heavens, the work of thy fingers, the moon and the stars, which thou hast ordained;

What is man, that thou art mindful of him? and the son of man, that thou visitest him?

For thou hast made him a little lower than the angels, and hast crowned him with glory and honour.

Thou madest him to have dominion over the works of thy hands; thou hast put all things under his feet:

All sheep and oxen, yea, and the beasts of the field;

The fowl of the air, and the fish of the sea, and whatsoever passeth through the paths of the seas.

O Lord our Lord, how excellent is thy name in all the earth!

PSALM 8:3–5

When I consider thy heavens, the work of thy fingers, the moon and the stars, which thou hast ordained;

What is man, that thou art mindful of him? and the son of man, that thou visitest him?

For thou hast made him a little lower than the angels, and hast crowned him with glory and honour.

PSALM 8:3–5
Sunset by John Frederick Kensett, 1867.
SuperStock/SuperStock/Getty Images.

As noted earlier, this is a well-known and much loved psalm, among the most cited of all canonized scripture to show the dignity and divinity of the "son [and daughters] of man"—you and I, mortals, humankind—who were made just "a little lower than the angels" and stand preeminent in the creation of the cosmos (see page 49 for a discussion of the Hebraic rendering of "Elohim" in place of "angels"). Clearly this is the intended reading of the text and conveys both the awe and gratitude of the Psalmist who is considering One so glorified sharing a significant portion of that glory with mere mortals. All of us have taken heart that we could stand in such a favorable position before God as the most important of His creations. Jesus cited the second verse of this psalm to indicate that children, too, in their crying out praises unto Him in the temple, are inspired and stand with the angels even as "babes and sucklings."[208]

But as with so many of the psalms (and many other scriptures as well), this passage can be read at another level that, without losing the primary interpretation outlined above, can at the same time elevate it to a psalm about the Messiah.

Addressed as this psalm is to "O Lord our Lord," the Psalmist is focusing on a divine being from the outset, God the Father, as Him to whom prayers are addressed. Another name for the Father is "Man of Holiness."[209] With that title in mind, it is easy to hear a divine echo in the reference to "the son of man." Granted, this phrase is not capitalized and there are many scriptures that use the lowercase "son of man" to speak simply of mankind, the mortal sons and daughters of the human family. But having said that, there is nevertheless the undeniable hint of divinity that comes to the reader's mind whenever one hears the phrase "son of man," lowercase or uppercase, simply because Jesus applied the phrase so often to Himself. Little wonder that we would make this mental association, as the four New Testament writers of the Gospels use the title "Son of man" to apply to Jesus no fewer than eighty-five times! As such it would have to be considered perhaps the most common of all titles in the scriptures applied to Jesus and His mission.

With this second, additional reading of the psalm, what was earlier— and is—the praise of a common man or woman becomes praise of the Son of Man. It is Jesus whom God has made "a little lower than the angels [Elohim]" in mortality, and who, when His triumphant mission is completed, will be crowned with "glory and honor" on the right hand of His Father. It is ultimately Christ to whom the Father has given "dominion over the works of [His] hands." Surely it is only of Christ that it can truly be said that *all things* have been put "under his feet." He alone is master of ocean and earth and sky, to say nothing of the beasts of the field, the fowls of the earth, and the fish of the sea in the wide expanse of creation. The application of this psalm to Jesus is made directly and explicitly by the Apostle Paul in both his first epistle to the Corinthians and the epistle to the Hebrews.[210]

It is as inspiring as it is encouraging to read of Christ's exalted standing before God in the great order of the creation and then to realize that we—common men and women with all kinds of failings and shortcomings—are included in that great order in a way that underscores *our* divinity as well! Such a reading of Psalm 8 gives even greater meaning to the Apostle Paul's declaration to the Romans:

"The Spirit itself beareth witness with our spirit, that we are the children of God: and if children, then heirs; *heirs of God, and joint-heirs with Christ;* if so be that we suffer with him, that we may be also glorified together."[211]

PSALM 16

Preserve me, O God: for in thee do I put my trust.

O my soul, thou hast said unto the Lord, Thou art my Lord: . . .

The Lord is the portion of mine inheritance and of my cup: thou maintainest my lot.

The lines are fallen unto me in pleasant places; yea, I have a goodly heritage.

I will bless the Lord, who hath given me counsel: my reins also instruct me in the night seasons.

I have set the Lord always before me: because he is at my right hand, I shall not be moved.

Therefore my heart is glad, and my glory rejoiceth: my flesh also shall rest in hope.

For thou wilt not leave my soul in hell; neither wilt thou suffer thine Holy One to see corruption.

Thou wilt shew me the path of life: in thy presence is fulness of joy; at thy right hand there are pleasures for evermore.

This has sometimes been referred to as the Golden Psalm, or the Psalm of the Precious Secret. But with the perspective of both history and the gospel record, we find the answer to the "secret" of death's inevitability and the ever-reaching clutches of hell to be the redemption of the Lord Jesus Christ. Among the early Apostles, both Peter and Paul recognized this interpretation of what might have been David's fear about his own death and destruction but ultimately applies to Christ and, through Him, to all humankind.

On that first majestic day of Pentecost when the Holy Ghost poured out such great gifts upon the Church, Peter quoted this psalm with particular emphasis on verses 8 through 10. He uses this passage to testify of the resurrection of Christ. It is worth quoting at least part of Peter's passionate declaration at length. The portions of Psalm 16 that Peter quotes have been italicized for easy recognition, but the entire passage as recorded in Acts 2 is central to the testimony of this eyewitness of Christ's resurrection:

"Ye men of Israel, hear these words; Jesus of Nazareth, a man approved of God among you by miracles and wonders and signs, which God did by him in the midst of you, as ye yourselves also know:

"Him, being delivered by the determinate counsel and foreknowledge of God, ye have taken, and by wicked hands have crucified and slain:

"Whom God hath raised up, having loosed the pains of death: because it was not possible that he should be holden of it.

"For David speaketh concerning him, *I foresaw the Lord always before my face, for he is on my right hand, that I should not be moved:*

"*Therefore did my heart rejoice, and my tongue was glad; moreover also my flesh shall rest in hope:*

"*Because thou wilt not leave my soul in hell, neither wilt thou suffer thine Holy One to see corruption. . . .*

"Men and brethren, let me freely speak unto you of the patriarch

David, that he is both dead and buried, and his sepulchre is with us unto this day.

"Therefore being a prophet, and knowing that God had sworn with an oath to him, that of the fruit of his loins, according to the flesh, he would raise up Christ to sit on his throne;

"He seeing this before spake of the resurrection of Christ, that his soul was not left in hell, neither his flesh did see corruption.

"This Jesus hath God raised up, whereof we all are witnesses."[212]

Later in the book of Acts, the Apostle Paul quotes both Psalm 2 and Psalm 16 in testifying of the resurrection of Christ. Again, the relevant quotes from the psalms are in italics:

"And we declare unto you glad tidings, how that the promise which was made unto the fathers,

"God hath fulfilled the same unto us their children, in that he hath raised up Jesus again; as it is also written in the second psalm, *Thou art my Son, this day have I begotten thee.*

"And as concerning that he raised him up from the dead, now no more to return to corruption, he said on this wise, I will give you the sure mercies of David.

"Wherefore he saith also in another psalm, *Thou shalt not suffer thine Holy One to see corruption.*

"For David, after he had served his own generation by the will of God, fell on sleep, and was laid unto his fathers, and saw corruption:

"But he, whom God raised again, saw no corruption."[213]

Clearly the early Apostles, to say nothing of David himself, saw the Resurrection of Jesus as not only the great distinguishing characteristic of Jesus' ministry but also the hope each of us has that we will be preserved by our trust in God's grace.[214] It is in the Father and the Son that we have our inheritance and we are maintained.[215] In them we have a goodly heritage and from them we receive counsel.[216] For these reasons we have the image of divinity always before us. Because godly strength is always with us, we shall not be moved.[217] For this certainty our heart is glad and our "flesh also shall rest in hope."[218] The promise of the Resurrection and the salvation it symbolizes brings a fulness of joy; Christ stands at the right hand of God,[219] and in Him "are pleasures for evermore."[220]

PSALM 21

The king shall joy in thy strength, O Lord; and in thy salvation how greatly shall he rejoice!

Thou hast given him his heart's desire, and hast not withholden the request of his lips. . . .

For thou preventest him with the blessings of goodness: thou settest a crown of pure gold on his head.

He asked life of thee, and thou gavest it him, even length of days for ever and ever.

His glory is great in thy salvation: honour and majesty hast thou laid upon him.

For thou hast made him most blessed for ever: thou hast made him exceeding glad with thy countenance.

For the king trusteth in the Lord, and through the mercy of the most High he shall not be moved.

In this psalm, like so many others, the image of the king is used to link the earthly rule of one like David with Christ, the King of kings. However much a mortal ruler might have blessings from heaven, it is Jesus to whom the Father will ultimately give "his heart's desire," not withholding anything from "the request of his lips." It is Jesus who personifies the "blessings of goodness" and who at the conclusion of His mortal mission would figuratively have "a crown of pure gold" placed upon His head. It is Jesus upon whom "glory" and "honour" and "majesty" have been placed. Surely it is Jesus who is "most blessed for ever," and in His devotion and integrity He "shall not be moved" from the truths He embodies and the witness of the Father He has borne.

PSALM 45

Thou art fairer than the children of men: grace is poured into thy lips: therefore God hath blessed thee for ever.

Gird thy sword upon thy thigh, O most mighty, with thy glory and thy majesty.

And in thy majesty ride prosperously because of truth and meekness and righteousness. . . .

Thy throne, O God, is for ever and ever: the sceptre of thy kingdom is a right sceptre.

Thou lovest righteousness, and hatest wickedness: therefore God, thy God, hath anointed thee with the oil of gladness above thy fellows.

All thy garments smell of myrrh, and aloes, and cassia, out of the ivory palaces, whereby they have made thee glad.

The Messiah is described here as being "fairer than the children of men." References to "grace," "glory," "majesty," "truth," "meekness," and "righteousness" all invoke images of and the qualities in the Savior of the world. Furthermore, doctrinal language such as that in verses 6 and 7—"Thy throne, O God, is for ever and ever: the sceptre of thy kingdom is a right sceptre" and "Thou lovest righteousness"—contains an echo of the inspiring language the Prophet Joseph Smith used in the depths of Liberty Jail wherein he noted "that the rights of the priesthood are inseparably connected with the powers of heaven, and that the powers of heaven cannot be controlled nor handled only upon the principles of righteousness." Then, if one understands this principle and lives for the realization of its promise, "The Holy Ghost shall be thy constant companion, and thy scepter an unchanging scepter of righteousness and truth; and thy dominion shall be an everlasting dominion, and without compulsory means it shall flow unto thee forever and ever."[221]

In his remarkable epistle to the Hebrews, Paul introduces that correspondence with a long, powerful testimony of Jesus Christ in which he quotes, among other verses of scripture, this psalm—specifically verses 6 and 7 cited above, plus the reference to being anointed "with the oil of gladness."[222]

When we are struggling and downtrodden, what an encouraging, hopeful thing it is to know we will be "glad" again. The holy priesthood carries with it wonderful covenantal promises. The Holy Ghost seals those expressions in the role of the Holy Spirit of Promise. All of these promises are to make the gifts of the gospel fully efficacious—and fully realized—in our lives. "Men are, that they might have joy."[223]

What a wonderful thought that in the end we might, with Christ, be anointed "with the oil of gladness," to be truly happy forever, almost as it were with a priesthood ordinance to that effect.

PSALM 68

Let the righteous be glad; let them rejoice before God: yea, let them exceedingly rejoice.

Sing unto God, sing praises to his name: extol him that rideth upon the heavens by his name JAH, and rejoice before him.

A father of the fatherless, and a judge of the widows, is God in his holy habitation.

God setteth the solitary in families: he bringeth out those which are bound with chains: but the rebellious dwell in a dry land.

O God, when thou wentest forth before thy people, when thou didst march through the wilderness. . . .

The earth shook, the heavens also dropped at the presence of God: even Sinai itself was moved at the presence of God, the God of Israel.

Thou, O God, didst send a plentiful rain, whereby thou didst confirm thine inheritance, when it was weary.

Thy congregation hath dwelt therein: thou, O God, hast prepared of thy goodness for the poor.

The Lord gave the word: great was the company of those that published it. . . .

The chariots of God are twenty thousand, even thousands of angels: the Lord is among them, as in Sinai, in the holy place.

Thou hast ascended on high, thou hast led captivity captive: thou hast received gifts for men; yea, for the rebellious also, that the Lord God might dwell among them.

Blessed be the Lord, who daily loadeth us with benefits, even the God of our salvation. . . .

He that is our God is the God of salvation; and unto God the Lord belong the issues from death. . . .

Sing unto God, ye kingdoms of the earth; O sing praises unto the Lord; . . .

To him that rideth upon the heavens of heavens, which were of old; lo, he doth send out his voice, and that a mighty voice.

Ascribe ye strength unto God: his excellency is over Israel, and his strength is in the clouds.

O God, thou art terrible out of thy holy places: the God of Israel is he that giveth strength and power unto his people. Blessed be God.

This is a particularly specific Messianic psalm in that verse 4 refers to "JAH," a variation of the more frequently rendered "yhwh" in Jewish literature. These are two of several abbreviated spellings of the name of God—traditionally "Jehovah" or the more literal transliteration "Yahweh"—the full spelling or enunciation of which was forbidden to the children of Israel. (The shorthand rule was to simply drop the vowels and leave enough identifying consonants for the reader to identify the figure being spoken of.) This is, of course, the premortal Jesus Christ, the God who delivers ancient Israel out of bondage in Egypt, and the "Lord" to which many of the Psalmist's prayers for personal or political deliverance are directed. In this regard, however, it is important to note that the Psalmist frequently appeals to Elohim. The word used for "God" in Genesis 1:1—"In the beginning God created the heaven and the earth," is a plural noun referring to "Gods" and is the traditional Latter-day Saint term for God the Father. Thus the singularly unified relationship of the Father and the Son is evident in the psalms and elsewhere in the Old Testament.[224]

In this psalm, "JAH" is the "father of the fatherless, and a judge of the widows," a God who "hast prepared of [His] goodness for the poor." Such phrases, of course, highlight elements that would become conspicuous in the teachings of Jesus when He came to minister in mortality. In reading such a passage, it is almost impossible not to think immediately of James's succinct definition of Christ's message: "Pure religion and undefiled before God and the Father is this, To visit the fatherless and widows in their affliction, and to keep himself unspotted from the world."[225]

Of course, even as "Sinai itself was moved at the presence of God, the God of Israel" (Jehovah), so will death and hell be "moved" by the presence and power of this same God, He who has and will "[lead] captivity captive." Paul would note this passage in his letter to the Ephesians, reassuring those readers there (exactly as the Prophet Joseph Smith did from Liberty Jail) that Christ would ascend up "far above all heavens" because He had paid the price to "[descend] first into the lower parts of the earth."[226] Truly "He that is our God is the God of salvation; and unto God the Lord belong the issues from death. . . . The God of Israel is he that giveth strength and power unto his people. Blessed be God."

PSALM 72

*Give the king thy judgments, O God, and thy righteousness
unto the king's son.*

*He shall judge thy people with righteousness, and thy poor
with judgment. . . .*

*He shall judge the poor of the people, he shall save the chil-
dren of the needy, and shall break in pieces the oppressor. . . .*

*In his days shall the righteous flourish; and abundance of
peace so long as the moon endureth.*

*He shall have dominion also from sea to sea, and from the
river unto the ends of the earth.*

*They that dwell in the wilderness shall bow before him; and
his enemies shall lick the dust. . . .*

*Yea, all kings shall fall down before him: all nations shall
serve him.*

*For he shall deliver the needy when he crieth; the poor also,
and him that hath no helper.*

*He shall spare the poor and needy, and shall save the souls of
the needy.*

He shall redeem their soul from deceit and violence: and pre-cious shall their blood be in his sight. . . .

His name shall endure for ever: his name shall be continued as long as the sun: and men shall be blessed in him: all nations shall call him blessed.

Blessed be the Lord God, the God of Israel, who only doeth wondrous things.

And blessed be his glorious name for ever: and let the whole earth be filled with his glory; Amen, and Amen.

This psalm is preeminent among a select few in the book for at least two reasons: First, it is one of the unknown number of psalms that we can assume really were written by David, and second, it demonstrates how the adoration of and supplication for an earthly king—in this case David's son Solomon—moves that earthly figure into a type or prefiguration of Christ, the Heavenly King. Many of the psalms fall into this category, with application both to mortal beings living in the immediate circumstance and to heavenly beings dwelling in eternity, but none of them demonstrate this literary and theological turn more clearly than does Psalm 72.

Note how the first line introduces this dual meaning and double level of reading in very few words. Clearly this introductory line is an appeal to God by "the king" (David) on behalf of "the king's son" (Solomon), but see how easily the reader is led to see this as typological, with God as "the king" and Jesus as "the king's son," especially when the word "judgments" is associated with the former and "righteousness" with the latter—traditional biblical characterizations of the Father and the Son.

With that introduction so skillfully laid as foundation, it is al-most impossible *not* to see Christ in the imagery for and about

Solomon that follows: He will judge all with "righteousness," but he will be especially mindful of "the poor" and "the needy." Under His rule "shall the righteous flourish" and there shall be an "abundance of peace" eternally ("so long as the moon endureth"). His dominion shall be global and His rule universal, "from sea to sea, and from the river unto the ends of the earth." Again special mention is made of the poor: "He shall deliver the needy when he crieth; the poor also, and him that hath no helper." And His deliverance will be spiritual as well as temporal. In sparing the poor in their economic plight, He will also "save the souls of the needy," redeeming them from deceit and violence, certainly two of the ancillary ills that so often accompany poverty. "Precious shall their blood be in his sight."

The psalm seems to move completely from earthly king to Heavenly King in its concluding verses. The imagery of Christ and His millennial reign is intentional:

> *His name shall endure for ever: his name shall be continued as long as the sun: and men shall be blessed in him: all nations shall call him blessed.*
>
> *Blessed be the Lord God, the God of Israel, who only doeth wondrous things.*
>
> *And blessed be his glorious name for ever: and let the whole earth be filled with his glory; Amen, and Amen.*

Some scholars believe—and the text would seem to indicate—that this may be the last of David's canonized psalms.[227] Whether it is or isn't, we can certainly say that it is one of the most Messianic of his psalms and in that regard could certainly serve well as a valedictory declaration regarding the Son of God who would one day come with the additional title of Son of David.[228]

PSALM 72:7–8

In his days shall the righteous flourish; and abundance of peace so long as the moon endureth.

He shall have dominion also from sea to sea, and from the river unto the ends of the earth.

PSALM 89

O Lord God of hosts, who is a strong Lord like unto thee? or to thy faithfulness round about thee?

Thou rulest the raging of the sea: when the waves thereof arise, thou stillest them. . . .

The heavens are thine, the earth also is thine: as for the world and the fulness thereof, thou hast founded them. . . .

Thou hast a mighty arm: strong is thy hand, and high is thy right hand.

Justice and judgment are the habitation of thy throne: mercy and truth shall go before thy face.

Blessed is the people that know the joyful sound: they shall walk, O Lord, in the light of thy countenance.

In thy name shall they rejoice all the day: and in thy righteousness shall they be exalted. . . .

For the Lord is our defence; and the Holy One of Israel is our king. . . .

He shall cry unto me, Thou art my father, my God, and the rock of my salvation.

Also I will make him my firstborn, higher than the kings of the earth. . . .

His seed also will I make to endure for ever, and his throne as the days of heaven. . . .

His seed shall endure for ever, and his throne as the sun before me.

It shall be established for ever as the moon, and as a faithful witness in heaven.

Similar to Psalm 72 just mentioned, this psalm also takes language applied either to a mortal leader (David) or to his God, and it gives the prayer additional meaning in terms of the Messiah who will later come as mortal and as divine. Consider, for example, a reference such as that in verse 9: "Thou rulest the raging of the sea: when the waves thereof arise, thou stillest them." Or verses 26–27: "He shall cry unto me, Thou art my father, my God, and the rock of my salvation. Also I will make him my firstborn, higher than the kings of the earth." Or verses 36–37: "His throne [shall endure] as the sun before me. It shall be established for ever as the moon, and as a faithful witness in heaven." All those passages have some meaning for mortal rulers, but they have special meaning in the life and ministry of Jesus and His eventual reign as King of kings and Lord of lords.

PSALM 102

But thou, O Lord, shalt endure for ever; and thy remembrance unto all generations.

Thou shalt arise, and have mercy upon Zion: for the time to favour her, yea, the set time, is come. . . .

So the heathen shall fear the name of the Lord, and all the kings of the earth thy glory.

When the Lord shall build up Zion, he shall appear in his glory.

He will regard the prayer of the destitute, and not despise their prayer.

This shall be written for the generation to come: and the people which shall be created shall praise the Lord.

For he hath looked down from the height of his sanctuary; from heaven did the Lord behold the earth;

To hear the groaning of the prisoner; to loose those that are appointed to death;

To declare the name of the Lord in Zion, and his praise in Jerusalem; . . .

Of old hast thou laid the foundation of the earth: and the heavens are the work of thy hands.

They shall perish, but thou shalt endure: yea, all of them shall wax old like a garment; as a vesture shalt thou change them, and they shall be changed:

But thou art the same, and thy years shall have no end.

This psalm has direct overtones of a latter-day/millennial time in which Zion's favored day arrives and "all the kings of the earth" shall acknowledge the the One True King, Jesus Christ, who will "appear in his glory." As always, this will be a King particularly mindful of the poor and the "destitute." In a very conspicuous way, a line like verse 20—that this Deliverer will "hear the groaning of the prisoner" and "loose those that are appointed to death"—echoes Isaiah's great Messianic passage (one of the greatest of all Messianic passages in the Old Testament) that begins: "The Spirit of the Lord God is upon me; because the Lord hath anointed me to preach good tidings unto the meek; he hath sent me to bind up the brokenhearted, to proclaim liberty to the captives, and the opening of the prison to them that are bound."[229]

These verses took on their greatest meaning—and fulfillment—when Jesus came to His childhood home of Nazareth, went into the synagogue on the Sabbath day, and read these words just cited from Isaiah 61, rendered this way in Luke 4: "The Spirit of the Lord is upon me, because he hath anointed me to preach the gospel to the poor; he hath sent me to heal the brokenhearted, to preach deliverance to the captives, and recovering of sight to the blind, to set at liberty them that are bruised."

With that He sat down, looked steadfastly at all in the synagogue (who were certainly all looking at Him!), and said to them, "This day is this scripture fulfilled in your ears."[230]

This was, of course, a public declaration of Jesus' Messiahship inasmuch as all in the synagogue—and virtually all in popular Jewish culture—would have recognized Isaiah's language (and the Psalmist's language behind that?), a verse long since understood to be applicable only to the Messiah when He would come in the flesh. The resulting fury among the listeners led them to rise up against Jesus and attempt to throw Him from the brow of the hill "headlong." But in a marvelous bit of scriptural understatement, Luke says only "But he [Jesus] passing through the midst of them went his way."[231]

PSALM 110

The Lord said unto my Lord, Sit thou at my right hand, until I make thine enemies thy footstool.

The Lord shall send the rod of thy strength out of Zion: rule thou in the midst of thine enemies.

Thy people shall be willing in the day of thy power, in the beauties of holiness from the womb of the morning: thou hast the dew of thy youth.

The Lord hath sworn, and will not repent, Thou art a priest for ever after the order of Melchizedek.

With the fairly common reference in the psalms of one Lord—the Father—speaking to another Lord—the Son—this passage places Christ on the traditional "right hand" of the Father,[232] a relationship that allows for the unity of the Father and the Son in every possible spiritual way but underscores the separateness of their physical being.

This psalm is also significant because it is one of only two places in the Old Testament where the great High Priest Melchizedek is mentioned by name—in this passage and in Genesis 14:18–20, wherein it is recorded that Abraham paid "tithes of all" to Melchizedek. The Apostle Paul quoted these verses from Psalm 110 not once but twice in his epistle to the Hebrews[233] in his effort to stress Christ's divine authority. These four citations are all that have survived in the Bible referring to this great high priest. Fortunately, Latter-day Saints know more than most about Melchizedek because of references to him in the thirteenth chapter of Alma in the Book of Mormon. Indeed, in that other "testament of Jesus Christ," Melchizedek is clearly a very specific Old Testament type for the Christ that was to come in New Testament times. It is noted that Melchizedek was "king over the land of [Jeru]Salem," "did reign under his father," "received the office of the high priesthood" in "the holy order of God," "did preach repentance unto his people," "did establish peace," and "was called the prince of peace"—all recognized by even the most casual of readers as characteristics of Jesus when He came in mortality.[234]

Because Melchizedek was such a great high priest—"there were many before him, and also there were many afterwards, but none were greater"[235]—his name was honored forever as the most noble substitute available for the name of the Son of God as it pertains to the holy priesthood. Section 107 of the Doctrine and Covenants, one of the greatest of all the revelations given in this or any day on the subject of the holy priesthood, begins:

"There are, in the church, two priesthoods, namely, the Melchizedek and Aaronic, including the Levitical Priesthood.

"Why the first is called the Melchizedek Priesthood is because Melchizedek was such a great high priest.

"Before his day it was called *the Holy Priesthood, after the Order of the Son of God.*

"But out of respect or reverence to the name of the Supreme Being, to avoid the too frequent repetition of his name, they, the

church, in ancient days, called that priesthood after Melchizedek, or
the Melchizedek Priesthood.

"All other authorities or offices in the church are appendages to
this priesthood."[236]

Once again the psalms make a contribution to our understanding
of the premortal Messiah that is as unique as it is important.

PSALM 118

O give thanks unto the Lord; for he is good: because his mercy endureth for ever. . . .

I called upon the Lord in distress: the Lord answered me, and set me in a large place.

The Lord is on my side; I will not fear: what can man do unto me?

The Lord taketh my part with them that help me. . . .

It is better to trust in the Lord than to put confidence in man.

It is better to trust in the Lord than to put confidence in princes. . . .

The Lord is my strength and song, and is become my salvation. . . .

The stone which the builders refused is become the head stone of the corner.

The concluding line of this psalm introduces what will become one of the most powerful and pervasive images of Christ running throughout all of scripture—Jesus as "the stone" who was rejected by His own, but who became "the head stone of the corner."

As with so many things Messianic, Isaiah took this image into majestic prophetic realms when he wrote:

"For the Lord spake thus to me. . . .

"Sanctify the Lord of hosts himself; and let him be your fear, and let him be your dread.

"And he shall be for a sanctuary; but for a stone of stumbling and for a rock of offence to both the houses of Israel, for a gin and for a snare to the inhabitants of Jerusalem.

"And many among them shall stumble, and fall, and be broken, and be snared, and be taken.

"Bind up the testimony, seal the law among my disciples. . . .

"Therefore thus saith the Lord God, Behold, I lay in Zion for a foundation a stone, a tried stone, a precious corner stone, a sure foundation: he that believeth shall not make haste."[237]

Paul uses this image extensively in such passages as 1 Corinthians 1:1:22–24:

"For the Jews require a sign, and the Greeks seek after wisdom:

"But we preach Christ crucified, unto the Jews a stumblingblock, and unto the Greeks foolishness;

"But unto them which are called, both Jews and Greeks, Christ the power of God, and the wisdom of God."

Consider, also, Ephesians 2:19–22:

"Now therefore ye are no more strangers and foreigners, but fellowcitizens with the saints, and of the household of God;

"And are built upon the foundation of the apostles and prophets, Jesus Christ himself being the chief corner stone;

"In whom all the building fitly framed together groweth unto an holy temple in the Lord:

"In whom ye also are builded together for an habitation of God through the Spirit."

However, none of the Apostles developed this scriptural metaphor more thoroughly than did Peter. He who would himself be called a "rock" knew firsthand the strength of Christ as the "stone of the corner" for the Church. In his majestic response to those who took him and his fellow Apostle John captive and who asked him, "By what power, or by what name, have ye done this?" ("this" being the healing of a lame man at the temple, bracketed by teachings which brought 3,000 and 5,000 souls, respectively, to the faith!), Peter, "filled with the Holy Ghost, said unto them, Ye rulers of the people, and elders of Israel,

"If we this day be examined of the good deed done to the impotent man, by what means he is made whole;

"Be it known unto you all, and to all the people of Israel, that by the name of Jesus Christ of Nazareth, whom ye crucified, whom God raised from the dead, even by him doth this man stand here before you whole.

"This is the stone which was set at nought of you builders, which is become the head of the corner.

"Neither is there salvation in any other: for there is none other name under heaven given among men, whereby we must be saved."[238]

Later, in his own canonized writings, Peter used this imagery again in testifying of Christ:

"To whom coming, as unto a living stone, disallowed indeed of men, but chosen of God, and precious,

"Ye also, as lively stones, are built up a spiritual house, an holy priesthood, to offer up spiritual sacrifices, acceptable to God by Jesus Christ.

"Wherefore also it is contained in the scripture, Behold, I lay in

Sion a chief corner stone, elect, precious: and he that believeth on him shall not be confounded.

"Unto you therefore which believe he is precious: but unto them which be disobedient, the stone which the builders disallowed, the same is made the head of the corner,

"And a stone of stumbling, and a rock of offence, even to them which stumble at the word, being disobedient: whereunto also they were appointed."[239]

But of course the most authoritative of all references to this image came from the Master Himself, the Great Stone of Israel. Following one of the most powerful of all parables about His coming—and His rejection—Christ made reference to Psalm 118 and said to those who opposed Him:

"Did ye never read in the scriptures, The stone which the builders rejected, the same is become the head of the corner: this is the Lord's doing, and it is marvellous in our eyes?

"Therefore say I unto you, The kingdom of God shall be taken from you, and given to a nation bringing forth the fruits thereof.

"And whosoever shall fall on this stone shall be broken: but on whomsoever it shall fall, it will grind him to powder.

"And when the chief priests and Pharisees had heard his parables, they perceived that he spake of them.

"But when they sought to lay hands on him, they feared the multitude, because they took him for a prophet."[240]

Truly Christ is the great "Rock of Heaven."[241] Not only did others say these things of Christ, but in His modesty and humility He said them of Himself. "Therefore whosoever heareth these sayings of mine, and doeth them, I will liken him unto a wise man, which built his house upon a rock: And the rain descended, and the floods came, and the winds blew, and beat upon that house; and it fell not: for it was founded upon a rock. And every one that heareth these sayings of mine, and doeth them not, shall be likened unto a foolish man, which built his house upon the sand: And the rain descended, and the floods came, and the winds blew, and beat upon that house; and it fell: and great was the fall of it."[242]

In our own lives, when the rains descend and the floods come and the winds blow, we can be more certain of this than of any other thing in the universe: Our faith in Christ, our foundation in Christ, our building on the rock of Christ will be a sure foundation that will withstand every grievance and every pain. He is the foundation whereon if we build, we cannot fall.

CRUCIFIXION AND ATONEMENT

As noted earlier, one of the moving realizations to which a reader of the psalms comes is in recognizing how frequently the Savior referred to them during His mortal ministry and how regularly the New Testament Gospel writers made use of the Old Testament Messianic psalms in testifying that Jesus was that Messiah. Furthermore, none of these many references are more poignant than those that came from or cast light upon the final hours of the Savior's life as He moved toward His crucifixion. Here are some of those references:

Psalm 41:9 "Yea, mine own familiar friend, in whom I trusted, which did eat of my bread, hath lifted up his heel against me."

With some of the saddest words ever written, this passage foretells Judas's treacherous betrayal of the Master. Of this incident (and of this passage) Jesus would say on the evening of the Last Supper, "I speak not of you all: I know whom I have chosen: *but that the scripture may be fulfilled, He that eateth bread with me hath lifted up his heel against me.*" Shortly thereafter Judas received the sop from Jesus' hand and "Satan entered into him. . . . [He] went immediately out: and it was night."[243] For Judas we fear it became night forever.

Psalm 69:4 "They that hate me without a cause are more than the hairs of mine head: they that would destroy me, being mine enemies wrongfully are mighty."

Earlier, Psalm 35 recorded, "Let not them that are mine enemies wrongfully rejoice over me: neither let them wink with the eye that hate me without a cause."[244] During His teaching time with the Twelve following the Passover meal of the Last Supper, Jesus said:

"He that hateth me hateth my Father also.

"If I had not done among them the works which none other man did, they had not had sin: but now have they both seen and hated both me and my Father.

"But this cometh to pass, that the word might be fulfilled that is written in their law, *They hated me without a cause*."[245]

Psalm 110:1 "The Lord said unto my Lord, Sit thou at my right hand, until I make thine enemies thy footstool."

As Jesus stood before Caiaphas and refused to answer his questions, the high priest raged and said, "I adjure thee by the living God, that thou tell us whether thou be the Christ, the Son of God." To this demand Jesus spoke His only words of the hour, "Thou hast said: nevertheless I say unto you, *Hereafter shall ye see the Son of man sitting on the right hand of power,* and coming in the clouds of heaven."[246]

Psalm 69:21 "They gave me also gall for my meat; and in my thirst they gave me vinegar to drink."

As the Roman soldiers prepared to crucify Jesus, it is recorded that "*They gave him vinegar to drink mingled with gall:* and when he had tasted thereof, he would not drink."[247]

Psalm 22:18 "They part my garments among them, and cast lots upon my vesture."

After the Roman soldiers took Jesus' clothing from Him and prepared to nail Him to the cross, John (who was present) writes:

"Then the soldiers, when they had crucified Jesus, took his

garments, and made four parts, to every soldier a part; and also his coat: now the coat was without seam, woven from the top throughout.

"They said therefore among themselves, Let us not rend it, but cast lots for it, whose it shall be: *that the scripture might be fulfilled, which saith, They parted my raiment among them, and for my vesture they did cast lots.* These things therefore the soldiers did."[248]

Psalm 22:16–17 "The assembly of the wicked have inclosed me: they pierced my hands and my feet. I may tell all my bones: they look and stare upon me."

Matthew records of these terrible hours, "They crucified him . . . and sitting down *they watched him there.*"[249]

Psalm 22:7–8 "All they that see me laugh me to scorn: they shoot out the lip, they shake the head, saying, He trusted on the Lord that he would deliver him: let him deliver him, seeing he delighted in him."

Matthew records, "And they that passed by *reviled him, wagging their heads,* and saying . . . save thyself. If thou be the Son of God, come down from the cross. Likewise also the chief priests *mocking him,* with the scribes and elders, said, *He saved others; himself he cannot save.* If he be the King of Israel, let him now come down from the cross, and we will believe him. . . . The thieves also, which were crucified with him, *cast the same in his teeth.*"[250]

Psalm 22:1–2 "My God, my God, why hast thou forsaken me? why art thou so far from helping me, and from the words of my roaring? O my God, I cry in the daytime, but thou hearest not; and in the night season, and am not silent."

This verse contains the most excruciating utterance in the Savior's atoning ordeal, perhaps the most excruciating cry in history. Matthew reminds us of this lowest point of anguish in the whole of the Crucifixion: "Now from the sixth hour there was darkness over all the land unto the ninth hour. And about the ninth hour Jesus cried with a loud voice, saying, Eli, Eli, lama sabachthani? that is to say, *My God, my God, why hast thou forsaken me?*"[251]

Psalm 22:14–15 "I am poured out like water, and all my bones are out of joint: my heart is like wax; it is melted in the midst of my bowels. My strength is dried up like a potsherd; and my tongue cleaveth to my jaws; and thou hast brought me into the dust of death."

John records the physical need the Savior experienced during the Crucifixion, "After this, Jesus knowing that all things were now accomplished, *that the scripture might be fulfilled, saith, I thirst.* Now there was set a vessel full of vinegar: and they filled a spunge with vinegar, and put it upon hyssop, and put it to his mouth."[252]

Psalm 31:4–5 "Pull me out of the net that they have laid privily for me: for thou art my strength. Into thine hand I commit my spirit: thou hast redeemed me, O Lord God of truth."

Luke records what is perhaps the most welcome cry of the long and indescribable Crucifixion ordeal: "And it was about the sixth hour, and there was a darkness over all the earth until the ninth hour. And the sun was darkened, and the veil of the temple was rent in the midst. And when Jesus had cried with a loud voice, he said, *Father, into thy hands I commend my spirit:* and having said thus, he gave up the ghost."[253]

Psalm 34:19–20 "Many are the afflictions of the righteous: but the Lord delivereth him out of them all. He keepeth all his bones: not one of them is broken."

In his account of the Crucifixion, John would observe, "The Jews therefore, because it was the preparation, that the bodies should not remain upon the cross on the sabbath day, (for that sabbath day was an high day,) besought Pilate that their legs might be broken, and that they might be taken away.

"Then came the soldiers, and brake the legs of the first, and of the other which was crucified with him.

"But when they came to Jesus, and saw that he was dead already, *they brake not his legs:*

"But one of the soldiers with a spear pierced his side, and forthwith came there out blood and water.

"And he that saw it bare record, and his record is true: and he knoweth that he saith true, that ye might believe.

"For these things were done, that the scripture should be fulfilled, *A bone of him shall not be broken.*"[254]

It is a wrenching thing indeed to realize that the only supportive thing that can be said of those soldiers who witnessed the greatest act of love ever offered in the history of all mankind is that they did not break the Savior's bones. That was because, as noted by John, Jesus was already dead and therefore did not need to have the process of His death hastened by the accelerated asphyxiation that would have come by the standard practice of breaking the leg bone, an act which took away the victim's ability to relieve the constriction on his lungs by "standing up" on the nails driven into his feet.

From what then had Christ died? He died from the weight of sin and sorrow, of sickness and sadness, of all the woes and troubles of the world from Adam to the end of time. All that was morally wrong or personally painful or sorrowful in any way down through the annals of time was gathered up and placed upon Jesus' shoulders and upon His shoulders alone. He who was mighty to save did save, treading the winepress of the Atonement entirely alone.

As the Psalmist recorded Messianically, "Reproach hath broken my heart; and I am full of heaviness: and I looked for some to take pity, but there was none; and for comforters, but I found none."[255] *Reproach hath broken my heart.* This was the ultimate cause of His death.

It should be remembered, of course, that Jesus ultimately gave up

His life voluntarily. He had divine life within Him and as such, no man or force could take His life from Him. Nevertheless, "there was of necessity a direct physical cause of dissolution" for His death, as Elder James E. Talmage phrased it,[256] and that physical cause was an irreversibly injured heart.

His heart simply gave out from such pain, sorrow, and suffering. Cardiac failure had followed respiratory failure, with fluid—bloody water—oozing into the pleural space surrounding the lungs. That is why His chest cavity produced a mixture of blood and water when the soldier pierced His side with a spear. For all of His physical and spiritual suffering, Jesus had *not* been subjected to internal trauma or violence to the inner organs. As unspeakable as His redeeming pain was, it did not come from the kind of injuries that would, in other circumstances, have caused internal bleeding or amniotic discharge. No, this unique victim had died of a "broken" heart. "I am poured out like water, and all my bones are out of joint: my heart is like wax; it is melted in the midst of my bowels."[257]

Because of the singular significance and eternal consequence of this process of triumph over both death and hell, we—and every generation until Christ comes again—embraced from that moment on a new symbol of our covenant to sacrifice. Little lambs would not be offered anymore after the great Lamb of God had come. No, ours would be a different symbol, a more personal gift, one with deeper meaning than the Old Testament version had held. For us now the great gift of the Atonement, including the Resurrection, was to take its meaning from the cross of Christ. As the resurrected Savior said to the Nephites in the New World:

"Behold, I am Jesus Christ the Son of God. . . .

"I am the light and the life of the world. I am Alpha and Omega, the beginning and the end.

"And ye shall offer up unto me no more the shedding of blood;

yea, your sacrifices and your burnt offerings shall be done away, for I will accept none of your sacrifices and your burnt offerings.

"And *ye shall offer for a sacrifice unto me a broken heart and a contrite spirit*. And whoso cometh unto me with a broken heart and a contrite spirit, him will I baptize with fire and with the Holy Ghost. . . .

"Behold, I have come unto the world to bring redemption unto the world, to save the world from sin."[258]

The directive is repeated again in this last great dispensation:

"Yea, blessed are they whose feet stand upon the land of Zion, who have obeyed my gospel; for they shall receive for their reward the good things of the earth, and it shall bring forth in its strength.

"And they shall also be crowned with blessings from above, yea, and with commandments not a few. . . .

"*Thou shalt offer a sacrifice unto the Lord thy God in righteousness, even that of a broken heart and a contrite spirit.*"[259]

Given the Psalmist's preoccupation with Messianic types and shadows, it should not be surprising that he accurately anticipated this great sacrificial transition from the Old Testament law to the New Testament gospel. He declared, "Create in me a clean heart, O God; and renew a right spirit within me. Cast me not away from thy presence; and take not thy holy spirit from me. . . . For thou desirest not sacrifice; else would I give it: thou delightest not in burnt offering. *The sacrifices of God are a broken spirit: a broken and a contrite heart.* . . . The Lord is nigh unto *them that are of a broken heart; and saveth such as be of a contrite spirit.*"[260]

It would appear that the Psalmist had more insight into the ultimate latter-day symbol of our salvation, a symbol instituted only after the Crucifixion and Atonement were complete, than any other writer in biblical scripture—Old *or* New Testament.

SECTION 3

THE TWENTY-THIRD PSALM

PSALM 23

The Lord is my shepherd; I shall not want.

He maketh me to lie down in green pastures: he leadeth me beside the still waters.

He restoreth my soul: he leadeth me in the paths of righteousness for his name's sake.

Yea, though I walk through the valley of the shadow of death, I will fear no evil: for thou art with me; thy rod and thy staff they comfort me.

Thou preparest a table before me in the presence of mine enemies: thou anointest my head with oil; my cup runneth over.

Surely goodness and mercy shall follow me all the days of my life: and I will dwell in the house of the Lord for ever.

GREEN PASTURES,
STILL WATERS, AND THE
GOOD SHEPHERD

Not only is Psalm 23 the world's favorite psalm, but it is arguably the most familiar and most quoted scripture in all of canonized writ. Its opening line—for all intents and purposes its title—must surely rank among the most readily identified phrases in the English language. Furthermore, quite apart from the theology expressed, it is acknowledged to be one of the most beautiful song-poems ever written. It is beloved of Christians and Jews, young and old, believers and nonbelievers, the sure and the uncertain. If someone is going to memorize a full, albeit short, chapter of scripture, it will likely be this one.

What is there in this passage that is so compelling and so comforting to such a wide variety of readers? As one gifted Jewish rabbi has said (after decades of studying the psalms):

"In a mere fifty-seven words of Hebrew and just about twice that number in English translation, the author of the Twenty-third Psalm gives us . . . a more practical theology than we can find in many books. . . . If we are anxious, the psalm gives us courage and

202

we overcome our fears. If we are grieving, it offers comfort and we find our way through the valley of the shadow [of death]. If our lives are embittered by unpleasant people, it teaches us how to deal with them. If the world threatens to wear us down, the psalm guides us to replenish our souls. If we are obsessed with what we lack, it teaches us gratitude for what we have. And most of all, if we feel alone and adrift in a friendless world, it offers us the priceless reassurance that 'Thou art with me.'"[261]

For the Hebraic tradition, the use of sheep and shepherds in this psalm is probably the most readily identifiable imagery that could have been employed. Sheep were everywhere in the biblical world and they are everywhere in the scriptures. Job owned 14,000 sheep. King Solomon sacrificed 120,000 sheep at the dedication of the temple he built. Parables about or principles pertaining to sheep and shepherding are some of the most common teaching metaphors in the scriptures and, not surprisingly, a frequently recurring motif in the earliest Christian art. The portrayal of a youthful shepherd carrying a sheep on his shoulders in the Old Testament prefigures Christ-as-Shepherd in the New. Such sheep-related types and shadows of salvation permeate the sacred records clear back to Adam and Eve. Upon being cast out of the Garden of Eden, Adam was immediately taught regarding the Atonement of Jesus Christ and the saving symbolism of the Lamb of God—not only the first but presumably the most important truth he could receive in mortality. Cain and Abel brought fratricide into the world in an argument over the sacrifice of a sheep versus the offering of a less symbolic gift.[262]

Against that ancient backdrop of mortality, sacrifice, and a variety of trouble, the twenty-third psalm has universal appeal in the comfort it gives to those who have faced—or are still facing—these trials and tribulations of life. As someone only half humorously said, this psalm is for parents with rebellious children, for soldiers going to war, and for someone who is just getting out of jail. Whatever our need, it shows God personally and actively involved in our lives. "He maketh me . . . He leadeth me . . . He restoreth [me] . . . Thou art with me . . . Thou preparest [for me] . . . Thou anointest [me]." From start to finish the psalm features an attentive, active Father and a needy, receiving child.

It should be noted that the title of this psalm notwithstanding, midway through it the imagery shifts away from the pastoral. The first half of the passage speaks of a shepherd and his sheep. The second half speaks of a generous royal host who provides a lavish feast for his guest. As a flock, the sheep have a verdant pasture and still water; as guests, the visitors have the most abundant and generous banquet possible. In both circumstances there is peace and protection. Let's reflect upon the individual elements of this universally beloved psalm.

"THE LORD IS MY SHEPHERD"

The Psalmist's premise in this most beautiful of all scriptural poems is twofold: first, that as the prophet Isaiah once declared, we are all "like sheep." As such, we need a shepherd because in innocence or ignorance—but on occasion willfully and against counsel—we turn "every one to his own way" and as a result "have gone astray."[263] We wander here and scamper there, inspect this and nibble at that, until at some point we look up and realize we are either lost or about to be destroyed. We realize that we, or others who affect us, have done either something stupid or something wrong—which are so very often the same thing. We realize we desperately need help; we are in trouble and frantically look about for our shepherd, our defender, our savior.

That leads to the second half of the Psalmist's initial declaration: that the only sure and safe shepherd is the Lord Jesus Christ—YHWH, Jehovah, the Lord God of Israel, Alpha and Omega, the

Beginning and the End, the Great I Am, He who came into mortality as Jesus of Nazareth to rescue every sheep of the fold that wishes to be saved. As the psalms say elsewhere, "He is our god; and we are the people of his pasture, and the sheep of his hand."[264] Life will be quick to teach us that we are all going to need a shepherd "at all times and in all things, and in all places."[265] How loving and strong, how devoted and determined that shepherd is in His care will be the all-important issue of our lives, though that may not be as obvious as it should be until we are in peril. Of course, what we often fail to remember is that in a fallen world and with a tempter bent on destroying us, we are in peril all the time. Thank heaven—literally—that Christ is our protector. As the prophet Isaiah promised, when the Lord comes, "He shall feed his flock like a shepherd: he shall gather the lambs with his arm, and carry them in his bosom, and shall gently lead those that are with young."[266]

In this same regard, no Old Testament prophecy anywhere exceeds the Prophet Ezekiel's eloquent and inclusive declaration of Jehovah's mortal ministry as Shepherd and Savior.

"For thus saith the Lord God; Behold, I, even I, will both search my sheep, and seek them out.

"As a shepherd seeketh out his flock in the day that he is among his sheep that are scattered; so will I seek out my sheep, and will deliver them out of all places where they have been scattered in the cloudy and dark day.

"And I will bring them out from the people, and gather them from the countries, and will bring them to their own land, and feed them upon the mountains of Israel by the rivers, and in all the inhabited places of the country.

"I will feed them in a good pasture, and upon the high mountains of Israel shall their fold be: there shall they lie in a good fold, and in a fat pasture shall they feed upon the mountains of Israel.

"I will feed my flock, and I will cause them to lie down, saith the Lord God.

"I will seek that which was lost, and bring again that which was driven away, and will bind up that which was broken, and will strengthen that which was sick: but I will destroy the fat and the strong; I will feed them with judgment."[267]

When Christ did come in New Testament times, He reaffirmed the view of those Old Testament witnesses: "I am the good shepherd: the good shepherd giveth his life for the sheep.

"But he that is an hireling, and not the shepherd, whose own the sheep are not, seeth the wolf coming, and leaveth the sheep, and fleeth: and the wolf catcheth them, and scattereth the sheep.

"The hireling fleeth, because he is an hireling, and careth not for the sheep. . . .

"As the Father knoweth me, even so know I the Father: and I lay down my life for the sheep."[268]

Truly "Our Lord Jesus [is] that great shepherd of the sheep."[269] And as the Psalmist affirms, He is *my* shepherd—first-person possessive. Traditionally ancient Israel usually spoke of "our" God, which, for an entire people, was most appropriate. But this beloved psalm reminds us that God is also the God of individuals and that His watchcare is immensely personal. The Lord is *my* shepherd.

"I SHALL NOT WANT"

The reader immediately recognizes in this phrase at least two meanings for the word *want*. One is a state of deprivation or insufficiency. By that definition, if the sheep does not "want," it is not going without, is not lacking the elements essential for well-being. Furthermore, reading the word *shall* in the future tense, it means the needs of the sheep will be met, they will be protected from deprivation or destitution, in the days that are to come. In the spirit of the

Psalmist's fears and forebodings, this is the most reassuring and comforting interpretation of the phrase. Obviously this does not mean that there won't be hard times or lean years when financial resources are depleted or other personal or family needs go unmet for a time. But surely what is never to be lean or depleted is our faith—faith in God, faith in the future, faith that things will work out. The Lord has declared, "What I the Lord have spoken, I have spoken, and I excuse not myself; and though the heavens and the earth pass away, my word shall not pass away, but shall all be fulfilled."[270] We need to remember and believe always that "God is powerful to the fulfilling of all his words. For he will fulfil all his promises which he shall make unto you."[271] His promise is that we won't lack forever, we won't go without endlessly. His promise is that we are watched over and will be cared for if we will keep our eye single to Him and His glory.

That leads to the second, closely related but nevertheless slightly different definition of *want,* which is to desire or yearn for. This interpretation is best caught by the little girl in a Sunday School class who misquoted—or slightly improved—the psalm when she said, "The Lord is my shepherd. That's all I want." I hasten to acknowledge that we are to desire some things. Our culminating article of faith says, "If there is anything virtuous, lovely, or of good report or praiseworthy, we seek after these things."[272] Clearly, many things are noble, desirable, and worth pursuing.

But in the context of the psalms and the troubles we face in daily life, it seems obvious that the message here is we should not always be wanting something we don't have or forever yearning for what is not ours. In its worst form, this is covetousness or avarice or greed. But even in its milder form, it is unattractive and unproductive envy. Classic literature is filled with figures who set out in search of the Holy Grail or the conquest of worlds or a pot of gold at the end of the rainbow only to discover that their prize (and certainly their happiness) was lying within their reach all the time—in their own life or their own home or their own modest and simple circumstance. In that sense we surely suffer needlessly and excessively from wanting, wanting, wanting—especially if those desires are focused on worldly or unworthy things. God does encourage the quest for good things. He does want us to "hunger and thirst after righteousness."[273] But surely He must weary of our wanting so many of the things that "moth and rust doth corrupt."[274] In saying he would not want excessively or seek incessantly the things of the world, the Psalmist was anticipating Jacob's counsel in the Book of Mormon, "Wherefore, do not spend money for that which is of no worth, nor your labor for that which cannot satisfy."[275] I shall not want.

"HE MAKETH ME TO LIE DOWN IN GREEN PASTURES"

It is safe to assume that lying down in a green pasture is the perfect dream come true for a sheep—the good life as seen from the vantage point of woolly little four-legged animals. It even sounds pretty good to us some days. No task waiting to be completed. No danger from without or trouble from within. Beauty for the eye, bread (or at least grass!) for the body, tranquillity for the soul—peaceful nature all around.

What keeps a sheep from enjoying such a circumstance regularly and routinely? An experienced sheep rancher who has written on this subject suggested that at least four things keep a sheep from such peaceful repose: fear, friction with other sheep, harassment from pests, and hunger.[276]

None of us have to be particularly brilliant to recognize that here, too, we are very much like sheep. These are some of the same things that keep us from peace in our world. Fears of a thousand kinds, real or imagined, where faith has not been cultivated. Conflicts with family or friend or foe, almost all of which could be eliminated if the gospel of Jesus Christ were allowed to prevail. Petty, pesky, pesty little disturbances of no eternal consequence that nevertheless irritate and annoy. Temporal appetites that intrude upon and finally distract us from spiritual pursuits. If we desire peace and tranquillity in our lives, we need to anticipate, address, and overcome these kinds of intrusions. That is easier said than done, but we ought to work at this, thereby allowing us to spend as much time as we can enjoying the green pastures God would like to give us.

And just a word or two about the word *maketh*. Within the doctrine of agency and moral freedom, there isn't much that the Lord ever *makes* us do. He can make us be accountable for our actions. He can make us feel the consequence of sin. He can make the elements around us respond to His command, and He may *entice* us to do all manner of good. But in the day-to-day course of mortal life, He doesn't "make" us do anything independent of our own agency. So in what sense does He "make" us lie down in peace and tranquillity?

Perhaps at least part of the answer is in a different interpretation of *maketh*. Is it possible that the Psalmist is saying, "God *made* me *in order that* I could lie down in green pastures"? Is it possible that, as with so many gospel principles and divine teachings, we are being shown the ideal, the ultimate purpose of our lives? Even if on some days peace, tranquillity, and green pastures seem so very far away, does *maketh* mean that those promises nevertheless await me, that for those purposes and that peace I was ultimately created?

If we can remember who we really are as children of the living God, and can keep in mind the plan for our salvation and the truths that will finally lead us there, we will be able to trust in and keep pursuing the great celestial destinies of our lives, including that day when we will have no fears, no foes, only peace of mind and tranquillity of soul. For that end we have been made and toward that end we need to keep striving. He maketh me to lie down in green pastures.

"He leadeth me beside the still waters"

This phrase is, of course, one with and the other half of the earlier promise of green pastures for God's little ones. Even more than the sustenance of the grass, sheep (and all other animals) need the constant supply and vitality of life-giving water. Man or beast can live for a fairly extended time without food, but nothing can live very long without water. *Agua vita.* The water of life. Water is an absolutely essential element in our makeup, which may be at least one of the reasons that God has instituted it as the means through which we are baptized unto eternal life. "Except a man be born of water and of the Spirit, he cannot enter the kingdom of God," Jesus told Nicodemus,[277] and to the Samaritan woman at the well, He taught, "The water that I shall give . . . shall be . . . a well of water springing up into everlasting life."[278]

In what may be the earliest Christian church ever excavated (a third-century house-church at Dura-Europos in Syria), a painting of a shepherd was found centrally featured over the baptismal font in a specially constructed baptistry there. Looking down, as it were, upon those participating in this essential ordinance, the Good Shepherd was leading His sheep into the fold of salvation through the medium of living water. Thus, at several levels of interpretation, water is essential for our survival. We cannot live without it, and a loving shepherd will make sure we find it. He thirsted on the cross in order that we might never have to face a comparable thirst of body or soul. We ought to drink deeply of His living water and be eternally grateful for the never-ending fountainhead from which it flows.

In terms of the psalm's theme and that of this book, it is of course not to be overlooked that these are "still waters" to which God's lambs are led. No turbulence of anxiety and opposition here. No crashing waves of conflict or destructive breakers of travail. Any lamb would be justifiably fearful if these sources were always agitated or erupting.

PSALM 23:1–2

The Lord is my shepherd; I shall not want.

He maketh me to lie down in green pastures: he leadeth me beside the still waters.

We fear floods and rampaging rivers, and swimming far from shore frightens us too. Tsunamis, typhoons, and hurricanes—all generated at sea—leave a wider swath of destruction than virtually any other manifestation of nature's violence. We speak of being "under water" in a situation we can't handle or perhaps "drowning" in debt or self-pity or life's complexities. No, in order to obtain sustenance for body or soul, we need still waters, peaceful waters, calm waters. They are a synonym for safe surroundings. We are led to such a setting by the Good Shepherd. He leadeth me beside the still waters.

"HE RESTORETH MY SOUL"

It would be nice if life were so calm and consistent that we never had occasion to feel discouraged or depleted. If there were no tribulation in our lives, no difficult or taxing circumstances that consumed our spiritual and emotional capital, we would have little need for any restoration to our soul. But life isn't calm or consistent, and we all face times that drain us of strength. Fatigue is a debilitating fact for all of us. We all get tired. This is why we all need sleep, we all need a break from our routines, we all need a vacation, however brief or inexpensive it might be.

Certainly this is the reason God ordained a Sabbath. Rabbi Harold S. Kushner has written regarding Exodus 31:17: "In six days the Lord made heaven and earth and on the seventh day He rested and was refreshed." He notes that in Hebrew, the verbs that translate "rest" and "refreshed" are *shavat*, meaning "He stopped" (from which the word *Sabbath* comes) and *yinafash*, meaning literally "He got His soul back."[279]

If God needs rest and refreshing, needs to "get His soul back" (if only symbolically and as an example for us), then surely we do as well. Every one of us needs refueling, regeneration, encouragement, hope. Fortunately, God has structured life in ways that we can get these if we will. As noted, His water is "living water," water that shall be "a well of water springing up into everlasting life."[280] That is real renewal!

So, too, with the bread of life. The bread of mortal existence leaves us hungry, sometimes almost as soon as we have eaten it. Even the manna that came to the Israelites in the desert was not long-term or life-giving in the spiritual sense. But Christ as "the bread of life" is, was, and always will be. "I am the bread of life," Jesus taught. "He that cometh to me shall never hunger . . . for the bread of God is he which cometh down from heaven, and giveth life unto the world."[281] We get life and hope, sustenance and help from God. Only heaven can restore our souls and put our feet solidly back under us.

In this latter regard, Phillip Keller, an experienced sheep rancher, noted that an old English shepherd's term for a sheep that has turned over on its back and cannot get up again by itself is a "cast" sheep, or a "cast down" sheep.[282] Given a sheep's physiology—and maybe its psychology—it will lie there on its back, flailing away with its legs in the air, until it dies if help doesn't come quickly enough. Not only is a natural death a threat in this circumstance, but the sheep is also helpless, hapless prey for any predator that may be watching for just such an easy kill.

As a side comment, it may be interesting to note that a fat, healthy sheep is probably more vulnerable to casting than others— suggesting that ease and luxury may be as much a challenge as want and limitations. What happens is that a well-fed and perhaps long-fleeced sheep—one who is seemingly coming along just as an owner would want—may lie down and roll around a little to stretch out and relax. However, if in the joy of all this the center of gravity shifts a little too much and all four of the legs lose contact with the ground, the sheep is "cast." It is highly unlikely that the lighter weight of the legs, even churning in midair as they are, will be substantial enough to overcome the bulk of the sheep's girth, which is literally holding those legs upright. I am not sure Paul had a "cast" sheep in mind, but he may have had a prosperous, seemingly self-sufficient Christian in mind when he wrote, "Wherefore let him that thinketh he standeth take heed lest he fall."[283]

All of us have been "cast down" from time to time, and we know what it is like to cry and bleat, flail and fear without any apparent ability to help ourselves get back on our feet under our own power. Then, as we should always do, we look to God and plead for help in times of trouble. Because He is the Good Shepherd, He is always watching, always aware, always looking for the sheep that is cast down. He readily comes and provides living water and the bread of life, lifting us up and setting things right. He puts us on our feet again. He restoreth our soul. And don't be surprised if His assessment for the future suggests we shed a little satisfied weight and have some of that excess wool shorn. As with the Father Gardener, "every branch that beareth fruit, he purgeth it, that it may bring forth more fruit."[284] Life has its ups and downs, but the Good Shepherd will always seek us out, will help us, and as necessary will discipline us sufficiently that we don't find ourselves vulnerable again in the future. He restoreth my soul.

"HE LEADETH ME IN THE PATHS OF RIGHTEOUSNESS FOR HIS NAME'S SAKE"

Men, rivers, and sheep will often—usually—almost always— follow the path of least resistance. For the most part, it is wander here and stray there, just as the old song of yesteryear says, "doing what comes naturally." This tendency is at the heart of the problem of mortality. As King Benjamin said, "For the natural man is an enemy to God, and has been from the fall of Adam, and will be, forever and ever, unless he yields to the enticings of the Holy Spirit, and putteth off the natural man and becometh a saint through the atonement of Christ the Lord, and becometh as a child, submissive, meek, humble, patient, full of love, willing to submit to all things which the Lord seeth fit to inflict upon him, even as a child doth submit to his father."[285]

Substitute "Shepherd" for "the Holy Spirit" and "the Lord" in that verse—titles that are, in this case, interchangeable—and you have the essence of our psalm: "He leadeth me in the paths of righteousness for his name's sake." Just as with the "cast" sheep in the first half of the verse, we are reminded here also that we cannot make this journey on our own. We are not smart enough, we are not good enough, we are not strong enough. We need help and guidance. We need someone who knows the way.

I know of only one of the Proverbs that is repeated twice verbatim. Could that be for some less-than-subtle emphasis? It is Proverbs 14:12, repeated again as 16:25: "There is a way that seemeth right unto a man, but the end thereof are the ways of death." Contrast that with Jesus' reassuring declaration, "I am the way, the truth, and the life: no man cometh unto the Father, but by me."[286] Repeatedly—as much as any other invitation in scripture—Christ invites us to follow Him, to come where He is, to do what He does, to go where He goes, to dwell where He dwells. Whatever path He is on is the path we should be on. Whatever path He marks is the path of righteousness. In the greatest psalm recorded in the Book of Mormon, Nephi cries, "O Lord, wilt thou not shut the gates of thy righteousness before me, that I may walk in the path of the low valley, that I may be strict in the plain road! . . . Wilt thou make my path straight before me! Wilt thou not place a stumbling block in my way—but that thou wouldst clear my way before me, and hedge not up my way."[287] Christ knows the way because He has walked it. He knows the way because He is the Way.

And what of the phrase "for his name's sake"? Walking the straight and narrow path of righteousness, the way of Christ, is acknowledgment that "this is the way; and *there is none other way **nor name** given under heaven whereby man can be saved in the kingdom of God. . . . This is the doctrine of Christ.*"[288] Furthermore "the sake" of Christ's name becomes ever more important as the path of righteousness leads to the covenants and attendant ordinances leading to eternal life. A new name is almost always a key element in a new covenant.[289] Thus the name of Christ is central to the identification of His Church,[290] to baptism and confirmation within it,[291] to partaking of the sacrament of the Lord's supper,[292] to ordination to the priesthood,[293] to temple ordinances, and so forth. Truly it is in and through Christ's name's sake that the path of ultimate righteousness is pursued. Because His honor and reputation are on the line—"for his name's sake"—He keeps all promises to His covenant children, specifically the promise inherent in the very name Jehovah—"the Unchangeable One," "the Great I Am." As He promised Moses, so He promises all of us, "Certainly I will be with thee."[294] You can count on Him. His good name is at stake. He leadeth me in the paths of righteousness for His name's sake.

"YEA, THOUGH I WALK THROUGH THE VALLEY OF THE SHADOW OF DEATH, I WILL FEAR NO EVIL: FOR THOU ART WITH ME"

With this verse the psalm shifts from focusing on a Shepherd in the third person (he) to a Host and Benefactor in the second person (thou). In this transition the psalm becomes even more personal, more prayerful, more grateful. Now life moves beyond sheep and shepherding to something more human for the struggling man or sorrowing woman. Now we consider life, death, and the shadows that link those mortal experiences. It may be useful to note that it is a "valley" we walk through in dark times. A "valley" is, in terms of a very contemporary illness, a "depression," a low point or down spot in the terrain. No triumphant stand "high on the mountain top" here.[295] No, we are down and maybe nearly out. And even to look up often reveals only that there is such a very long way to go.

We are forced in our mortality to acknowledge how much darkness there truly is in the world and how much of it we have to confront, sometimes almost daily. But ringing from this greatest of all reassuring psalms is the promise that these telestial tribulations are not ultimately final nor permanently fatal. Even though earthly life does end in death, we walk *through* that shadow and any of the evils (or merely natural realities) that led to it, emerging safely on the other side of the experience. Why? Because God is with us—in life, in death, and on through to eternal life.

That leads us to remember that there is another aspect of a "valley" that must not be forgotten. Almost by definition valleys are more verdant, more bountiful, more luxurious and peaceful than much that surrounds them on more rocky and rugged slopes nearby. If there is any water running down from those slopes, it is bound to run through the valley on its way down from the mountains to the sea. And entering into a valley also means that we don't have to climb for a while, that things have eased up a bit, that we can rest and renew, take a deep breath and summon strength before climbing again. The early pioneers traveling west always looked forward to the day—and certainly rejoiced in it when it came—that they could enter the valley. That image, that goal, was what kept many a man walking and many a woman believing.

Whether it is a bad day or good, dark moment or happy, verdant valley or one overshadowed with the reality of evil and threat of death, we "will fear no evil: for thou art with [us]." Often simple companionship will suffice when no other explanation of life's pain will do. When my infant brother died, I remember the comfort provided by those who came to our home just to sit silently with my parents. Words were essentially useless. Just being with us was the best gift they could have given. In that spirit, Psalm 56, with which we began these reflections, gives the single greatest reassurance that can be given in scripture, whatever the nature of our valley: "When I cry unto thee, then shall mine enemies turn back: this I know; for God is for me."[296] He is with us in life and He is with us in death. He is with us in sunshine and He is with us in shadow. He overcomes evil because He is the personification of goodness. He is the Resurrection and the Life. No evil can offset the Atonement of Jesus Christ, and no death can triumph over the victory that is His. The sun/Son *always* rises. Wherever we walk and whatever we face, we have nothing to fear—ever. Yea, though I walk through the valley of the shadow of death, I will fear no evil: for thou art with me.

"THY ROD AND THY STAFF THEY COMFORT ME"

In ancient days the only instruments a shepherd carried were a rod and a staff. The rod was a short, stout, club-like weapon used to defend oneself or the flock from an intruder. It was meant to be— and to convey—strength and power in the hand of a strong shepherd who knew how to use it. Of course, in a more theological way, the "rod" God uses to protect us and drive back the enemy is His mouth and the words of eternal counsel that flow from it. When necessary, those words and that mouth can be very forceful indeed. "But with righteousness shall he judge the poor, and reprove with equity for the meek of the earth: and he shall smite the earth with the rod of his mouth, and with the breath of his lips shall he slay the wicked," wrote the prophet Isaiah.[297] The words—and the Word—of God will truly be a comfort to the faithful, but to the ungodly they will be an instrument of condemnation.

The staff was a longer, lighter piece, usually with a hook (or crook) on the end used for rescuing a stranded sheep. It, more than the rod, is associated in both art and myth with the shepherd and his vigilant watchcare. Anyone who has ever seen a Primary class's reenactment of the Nativity is sure to recognize the shepherds by their ever-present staffs. Interestingly enough, in addition to being an extension of the shepherd's loving arm in either rescuing an errant sheep or guiding it in a new direction, the staff is also a means of support for the shepherd, a strength against which the weary walker can lean. Everything about the staff speaks of safety and care. It is the great scriptural instrument of rescue and redemption.

In life we need defending and we need rescue. One way or the other, we are vulnerable. Whether it be in threatening confrontations or routine wandering, we are blessed and protected by God's vigilant care. Thy rod and thy staff they comfort me.

"THOU PREPAREST A TABLE BEFORE ME IN THE PRESENCE OF MINE ENEMIES"

Notice again that although the sheep/shepherd theme continues to a degree, we are now speaking of a royal banquet table set for human consumption and human delight. Unfortunately, there are enemies nearby (and truly God's people, especially the youth among us, are always living in enemy territory), but in spite of that, a beautiful array is set, and those enemies are not allowed to come near to the feast nor to interrupt the favored guest. This Host has the bounty to feed and the power to protect. His guest is to eat and drink in peace. There is a sense of invulnerability here that is greatly to be desired in times of trouble.

Furthermore it should be noted that this banquet is apparently provided to the traveler without request or advance notice. The scene begs the recollection of Isaiah's great declaration of God's generosity:

"Every one that thirsteth, come ye to the waters, and he that hath no money; come ye, buy, and eat; yea, come, buy wine and milk without money and without price.

"Wherefore do ye spend money for that which is not bread? and your labour for that which satisfieth not? hearken diligently unto me, and eat ye that which is good, and let your soul delight itself in fatness."[298]

It should not be overlooked that one of the theological reasons the enemy is kept away from this festive, peaceful gathering is the righteousness of the people. The prophet Nephi noted:

"And he gathereth his children from the four quarters of the earth; and he numbereth his sheep, and they know him; and there shall be one fold and one shepherd; and he shall feed his sheep, and in him they shall find pasture.

"And because of the righteousness of his people, Satan has no power."[299]

The assurance of Christ's triumph over the adversary and over our imperfections. Unexpected. Unearned. (Sometimes unappreciated!) Always unbounded. That is the feast of salvation, the defeat of death, of hell, and of difficult days. In the final vision of things, John the Revelator notes that God's gracious hospitality in eternity is characterized as sitting down at the supper table of the Lamb.[300] That is the culminating image of the Atonement and redemption of Jesus Christ. To a weary and frightened wanderer, such splendor and relief must take the breath away. Thou preparest a table before me in the presence of mine enemies.

"THOU ANOINTEST MY HEAD WITH OIL; MY CUP RUNNETH OVER"

Some form of the word *anoint* appears nearly 200 times in scripture. In ancient times, perfumed oil was poured on the heads of guests at the feast of a distinguished host in the community. In those settings, the anointing suggested at the very least sanctity and respect. Often it implied a more formal covenantal relationship. In its ultimate significance, the anointing was part of a coronation, the bestowal of a kingship and a kingdom. All of these meanings are conveyed in the prophecy Isaiah made regarding the coming of the Messiah:

"The Spirit of the Lord God is upon me; because the Lord hath anointed me to preach good tidings unto the meek; he hath sent me to bind up the brokenhearted, to proclaim liberty to the captives, and the opening of the prison to them that are bound;

"To proclaim the acceptable year of the Lord, and the day of vengeance of our God; to comfort all that mourn;

"To appoint unto them that mourn in Zion, to give unto them beauty for ashes, the oil of joy for mourning, the garment of praise for the spirit of heaviness; that they might be called trees of righteousness, the planting of the Lord, that he might be glorified."[301]

This is, as mentioned earlier, the Messianic scripture Christ quoted in the synagogue in Nazareth that caused such furor when He said to those present, "This day is this scripture fulfilled in your ears."[302]

Later in the Savior's life this moving account recorded by Luke would further underscore a different kind of anointing of the Lord:

"And one of the Pharisees desired him that he would eat with him. And he went into the Pharisee's house, and sat down to meat.

"And, behold, a woman in the city, which was a sinner, when she knew that Jesus sat at meat in the Pharisee's house, brought an alabaster box of ointment,

"And stood at his feet behind him weeping, and began to wash his feet with tears, and did wipe them with the hairs of her head, and kissed his feet, and anointed them with the ointment.

"Now when the Pharisee which had bidden him saw it, he spake within himself, saying, This man, if he were a prophet, would have known who and what manner of woman this is that toucheth him: for she is a sinner.

"And Jesus answering said unto him, Simon, I have somewhat to say unto thee. And he saith, Master, say on.

"There was a certain creditor which had two debtors: the one owed five hundred pence, and the other fifty.

"And when they had nothing to pay, he frankly forgave them both. Tell me therefore, which of them will love him most?

"Simon answered and said, I suppose that he, to whom he forgave most. And he said unto him, Thou hast rightly judged.

"And he turned to the woman, and said unto Simon, Seest thou this woman? I entered into thine house, thou gavest me no water for my feet: but she hath washed my feet with tears, and wiped them with the hairs of her head.

"Thou gavest me no kiss: but this woman since the time I came in hath not ceased to kiss my feet.

"My head with oil thou didst not anoint: but this woman hath anointed my feet with ointment.

"Wherefore I say unto thee, Her sins, which are many, are forgiven; for she loved much: but to whom little is forgiven, the same loveth little.

"And he said unto her, Thy sins are forgiven.

"And they that sat at meat with him began to say within themselves, Who is this that forgiveth sins also?

"And he said to the woman, Thy faith hath saved thee; go in peace."[303]

Of course, the significance of the Psalmist's feeling that *his* (our) head can be anointed is because of Christ's gift to every one of us. Like the guest being so royally treated, we too have the chance for the divinely ordained life, for a destiny as kings and queens in the eternal realm. When we consider such blessings in this world and in the world to come, truly our chalice can't contain it; our "cup runneth over." Gratitude is the key to savoring all other gifts from God because without it, all other gifts seem insufficient or inadequate. Rather than complaining that life is hard or that our blessings don't seem abundant enough or that there are always thorns among the roses, shouldn't we be grateful that life, however difficult, is precious, that in addition we have the promise of eternal life, that the blessings we have are wonderful and those we will have are more wonderful yet, and that there are roses among the thorns? In the gospel of Jesus Christ, to quote a popular song, "everything is coming up roses." God's goodness overflows. Thou anointest my head with oil; my cup runneth over.

"SURELY GOODNESS AND MERCY SHALL FOLLOW ME ALL THE DAYS OF MY LIFE"

Unfortunately, the Psalmist does not say that in mortality our cup will *always* be full or that our heads will *always* be anointed with oil, but in this verse we do have the promise that even in a telestial sphere of trial and growth, God's goodness and mercy will *always* be with us. That means that, as the hymn says, His arms will be put "unfailingly round" us, for ever and ever, through thick or thin, through triumph or tragedy.[304] Indeed, apparently the Hebrew word translated as *follow* is something more like *pursue*. In that regard, one thinks of Francis Thompson's poem "The Hound of Heaven," in which the Lord "hounds" the Christian and won't rest until His prey stops running from grace, until he yields to God's love and his soul is saved.

Furthermore it should be noted that in this phrase *goodness* and *mercy* are used as personal nouns, not adjectives or mere descriptive virtues. Thus the line introduces for the first time in this psalm the promise of help from other divine beings besides the Lord. In the Hebraic tradition, a great deal has been written about the idea of two angels or special messengers that are dispatched by the Lord to watch over a special person or dignitary. They were to be ever watchful and never leave their person unattended. One distinguished scholar has gone so far as to say this was the scriptural introduction of the tradition that would develop into the idea of "guardian angels." The notion of two specifically assigned angels for each mortal person on earth is not part of our doctrine, but the reality of angelic watch-care is and will be our doctrine "so long as time shall last, or the earth shall stand, or there shall be one man [or woman] upon the face thereof to be saved."[305]

The message here is clear: Heavenly beings will, with goodness and mercy, care and compassion, strength and safety, watch over God's children day and night, in sickness and in health. This is the most important and most eternal meaning of this verse.

But there is another possible reading of the verse that we should also consider. It could mean—and seems consistent with Christian belief to mean—that after we have been treated so lovingly first by a Good Shepherd and then by a Royal Host, we should "go, and do . . . likewise" to others.[306] That is, if we are the recipients of such generosity and abundance, then those blessings should "follow us" or go with us, be evident in our association with others wherever we go, "all the days of [our] life." If we have been shown goodness, we should show goodness. If we have been dealt with mercifully, we should deal mercifully. Everywhere we go, people ought to be able to say, "I have been in the presence of a disciple of Christ. I felt goodness flowing from him. I found mercy at her hand. They live lives of compassion and love. These qualities seem to 'follow them' wherever they go."

One of the simplest summaries of Christ's life was that He "went about doing good."[307] Goodness "followed him." It ought to follow those who profess His name and call Him Master. Surely goodness and mercy shall follow me all the days of my life.

"I WILL DWELL IN THE HOUSE OF THE LORD FOR EVER"

This is a reference—as in so many of the psalms—to the holy temple. The significance of temple ordinances in God's plan for His sons and daughters cannot be overstated. All roads in the gospel lead to the house of the Lord (or, as in this beautiful psalm, *back* to the house of the Lord), which house is already halfway to heaven. Thus the temple is the great intersection of time and eternity. In our instruction from and communion with the divine there, we learn powerfully and poignantly who we really are, where we were before we came here, why it was crucial for us to come into mortality, and what our destiny can be forever if we embrace and live the gospel truths taught, particularly as they pertain to the Atonement of Jesus Christ.

This pursuit of personal exaltation takes on added importance when in the course of our earthly sojourn we come to understand the significance of the eternal family. In the temple we learn—again— that we are literally the spiritual offspring of God, with eternal ties to Him and to each other and special promises regarding the continuity of family relationships beyond the grave. Of those who are "bone of [our] bones, and flesh of [our] flesh,"[308] a modern prophet has asked, "Was there ever a man who truly loved a woman, or a woman who truly loved a man, who did not pray that their relationship might continue beyond the grave? Has a child ever been buried by parents who did not long for the assurance that their loved one would again be theirs in a world to come? Can anyone believing in eternal life doubt that the God of heaven would grant his sons and daughters that most precious attribute of life, the love that finds its most meaningful expression in family relationships? No, reason demands that the family relationship shall continue after death. The human heart longs for it. The God of heaven has revealed a way whereby it may be secured. The sacred ordinances of the house of the Lord provide for it."[309]

Because the temple is characterized by such sacred promises, such holiness and divine safety, it has always been a place of refuge in our times of trouble, a fortress for covenantal communion when our needs are great. Here in this most consecrated of edifices, this most sacred space on earth, God figuratively (and one day literally) comes to greet us, endow us, embrace us, and seal us His. In response, we strive—within its precincts and without—to lift ourselves out of the worldly ills and damaging influences of mortality, to reach up to celestial possibilities, to be our best spiritual selves with a "brightness of hope, and a love of God and of all men."[310] Such revelation and renewal, courage and peace are at their brightest and best within the sanctuary of the Lord. Little wonder that Jesus' most furious acts in mortality were in response to the desecration of the temple and its consecrated purposes. And little wonder that the Psalmist finds such sweet satisfaction in entering there, never to go beyond its comfort and protection again. John the Revelator envisioned such an ultimate opportunity for all of us: "What are these which are arrayed in white robes? and whence came they? . . . These are they which came out of great tribulation, and have washed their robes, and made them white in the blood of the Lamb. Therefore are they before the throne of God, and serve him day and night in his temple."[311] I will dwell in the house of the Lord for ever.

As we close this psalm (and this book about the psalms), it should be noted that the Lord (Yahweh) begins this prayerful song—"the Lord is my shepherd"—and the Lord (Yahweh) concludes it—"in the house of the Lord for ever." Although the name of Jehovah is not used anywhere else in the twenty-third psalm, it is clear from start to finish that He is the Good Shepherd spoken of and He is the generous, royal host.

As in this psalm, so too should it be in our lives. He should be our beginning and our end. He should be our first and our last. He should be our Alpha and Omega. "The God of all comfort," as the Apostle Paul so lovingly describes Him,[312] should bracket our experience every day and every night. As Alma of old pled with his son, "Cry unto God for all thy support; yea, let all thy doings be unto the Lord, and whithersoever thou goest let it be in the Lord; yea, let all thy thoughts be directed unto the Lord; yea, let the affections of thy heart be placed upon the Lord forever. Counsel with the Lord in all thy doings, and he will direct thee for good; yea, when thou liest down at night lie down unto the Lord, that he may watch over you in your sleep; and when thou risest in the morning let thy heart be full of thanks unto God; and if ye do these things, ye shall be lifted up at the last day."[313]

Our hopes and our dreams. Our beginning and our end. Our past, our present, and our future should all be characterized by our proximity to and adoration for Him whose flock we are and whose royal guests we should wish to be—in times of trouble and always.

PSALM 23:6

Surely goodness and mercy shall follow me all the days of my life: and I will dwell in the house of the Lord for ever.

NOTES

SECTION I
REFLECTIONS

1. William Shakespeare, *Hamlet,* act 3, scene 1, line 60.

2. See Harold S. Kushner, *The Lord Is My Shepherd: Healing Wisdom of the Twenty-Third Psalm* (2003), 102.

3. 2 Nephi 2:11.

4. See Malachi 4:2; 2 Nephi 25:13; 3 Nephi 25:2.

5. Psalm 22:11.

6. Psalm 25:16–18.

7. Psalm 69:1–3, 14–17.

8. Psalm 107:26–31.

9. See Thomas Paine, *The American Crisis* (1819), 16.

10. C. Hassell Bullock, *Encountering the Book of Psalms* (2001), 15.

11. Luke 24:44–45; emphasis added.

12. This elevated status for the psalms is also suggested in the generally accepted division of the collection into five parts (1–41, 42–72, 73–89, 90–106, 107–150), intentionally reminiscent of the division of the five books of Moses.

13. Professor John W. Welch of Brigham Young University has written definitively on this subject in his book *The Sermon on the Mount in the Light of the Temple* (2009).

14. Psalm 1:1; emphasis added.

15. Matthew 5:1.

16. Isaiah 2:3.

17. Matthew 5:8.

18. The Septuagint is the Hebrew Bible as it was translated into the Greek language in the third to first centuries B.C. It is so named because seventy Jewish translators did the work. The Apostle Paul and the early Church Fathers frequently quoted from the Septuagint.

19. For a further examination of this psalmic link to the Beatitudes, see Andrew C. Skinner, "Israel's Ancient Psalms: Cornerstone and the Beatitudes," in *The Sermon on the Mount in Latter-day Scripture* (2010).

The psalm itself is discussed in more detail on pages 57–59 of this book.

20. Matthew 5:5.

21. Alma 42:25.

22. Romans 8:31, 37.

23. See 1 Nephi 8.

24. John 14:6.

25. See Genesis 39:7–12.

26. Alma 8:14–15.

27. John 4:35.

28. William Shakespeare, *Macbeth,* act 2, scene 2, line 37.

29. Isaiah 30:15.

30. Isaiah 40:28–31.

31. Job 38:2, 4, 6, 8, 11.

32. Job 40:8.

33. Job 40:9.

34. Job 42:3, 6.

35. D&C 5:34.

36. D&C 123:17.

37. Robert D. Hales, "Waiting upon the Lord: Thy Will Be Done," *Ensign,* November 2011, 72–73.

38. Psalm 4:4.

39. William Wordsworth, "Personal Talk," in *The New Oxford Book of English Verse,* chosen and edited by Helen Gardner (1972), 507.

40. *Teachings of Presidents of the Church: David O. McKay* (2003), 31–32.

41. 2 Nephi 2:25.

42. Isaiah 55:1.

43. John Donne's Sermons, no. 28.

44. D&C 121:3.

45. Psalm 13:1.

46. D&C 121:1–3.

47. D&C 121:7.

48. D&C 121:9.

49. D&C 121:10.

50. 2 Nephi 33:3.

51. Revelation 21:4.

52. 3 Nephi 17:21–23.

53. 3 Nephi 26:14, 16.

54. 3 Nephi 26:14.

55. Alma 32:23.

56. Matthew 19:14.

57. William Wordsworth, "Ode: Intimations of Immortality from Recollections of Early Childhood," in *New Oxford Book of English Verse,* 509.

58. Matthew 14:23.

59. Luke 4:42.

60. Mark 1:35–37.

61. Luke 6:11–12.

62. *Lectures on Faith* (1985), 72–73; emphasis added.

63. D&C 63:64.

64. Ecclesiasticus 28:17.

65. An alternate translation from the Greek.

66. James 3:2–10; emphasis added.

67. Ephesians 4:29–32.

68. Helaman 5:12.

69. 1 Samuel 2:2.

70. D&C 6:34.

71. Mosiah 24:15.

72. Alma 30:44.

73. Moses 1:33.

74. C. S. Lewis, *The Weight of Glory* (HarperCollins: 2001), 45.

75. "Come unto Him," *Hymns of The Church of Jesus Christ of Latter-day Saints* (1985), no. 114.

76. Hebrews 6:6.

77. Articles of Faith 1:4.

78. Matthew 16:19–21.

79. 1 Nephi 4:2.

80. "Come, Come, Ye Saints," *Hymns,* no. 30.

81. Moroni 7:48.

82. James 3:17.

83. D&C 43:14, 9.
84. D&C 58:42.
85. John 2:16; see also Matthew 21:13.
86. See 1 Corinthians 13:13.
87. Ecclesiastes 1:5.
88. Revelation 22:16.
89. See John 12:24.
90. D&C 59:8.
91. William Congreve, *The Mourning Bride,* act 1, scene 1, lines 1–2.
92. "Come, Come, Ye Saints," *Hymns,* no. 30.
93. See Matthew 26:30.
94. See Moses 5:6–8.
95. See Luke 1:11–38.
96. See Matthew 2:13–23.
97. See, for example, Matthew 4:11; 28:2; Luke 22:43; 24:23.
98. Hebrews 13:2.
99. Moroni 7:35–37, 30.
100. See D&C 84:46.
101. See 1 Corinthians 15:40–42; also D&C 76:50–112.
102. Joseph Smith–History 1:16; emphasis added.
103. Mosiah 16:9.
104. Jacob 2:17–19.
105. 3 Nephi 14:20.
106. Alexander Pope, "An Essay on Criticism," part II (1709).
107. Exodus 20:17.
108. Romans 3:23.
109. See 1 Nephi 8:12–13.
110. See Enos 1:9, 11.
111. See Alma 5:19.
112. Psalm 12:5.
113. Exodus 23:11.
114. 1 Samuel 2:8.
115. Proverbs 17:5.

116. Proverbs 28:27.
117. Matthew 19:21.
118. Mosiah 4:19.
119. Mosiah 4:26.
120. Alma 1:27.
121. Alma 4:13.
122. Alma 5:55.
123. Alma 34:28.
124. Mormon 8:37.
125. D&C 42:31.
126. D&C 105:3.
127. Isaiah 3:15.
128. See Alma 33:3.
129. 3 Nephi 18:18; D&C 20:33; 61:39.
130. Alma 34:27.
131. Alma 37:36.
132. Alma 34:21.
133. Daniel 6:10.
134. D&C 52:14.
135. 3 Nephi 18:18.
136. "Sweet Hour of Prayer," *Hymns,* no. 142.
137. Martin Luther, "Before the Diet of Worms."
138. Job 27:3–5; 31:6.
139. "Come, Thou Fount of Every Blessing," *Hymns* (1948), no. 70.
140. Isaiah 22:23.
141. Acts 3:4, 6–7.
142. Harold B. Lee, "'Stand Ye in Holy Places,'" *Ensign,* July 1973, 123.
143. Moses 7:28, 29, 32, 37.
144. See, for example, John 11:35; 3 Nephi 17:14, 21–22.
145. See Luke 19:41–44.
146. Psalm 126:5.
147. D&C 6:33.
148. Ralph Waldo Emerson, "Experience," in *Essays: Second Series* (1841).

149. See 2 Nephi 2:25.

150. 2 Nephi 31:20.

151. Alma 42:16.

152. "Count Your Blessings," *Hymns,* no. 241.

153. This is why it is so important *not* to verbalize negative feelings and fears habitually. To give them undue expression is to give them a life they do not deserve.

154. Alma 34:38.

155. Psalm 78:8.

156. Joshua 4:5–7.

157. 2 Nephi 25:21–23, 27.

158. Moses 7:61.

159. Moses 7:62.

160. D&C 128:22–23.

161. Mark 4:37.

162. Mark 4:38.

163. Mark 4:39.

164. Mark 4:40–41.

165. "Master, the Tempest Is Raging," *Hymns,* no. 105.

166. D&C 1:38.

167. 1 Corinthians 12:21.

168. 2 Nephi 9:29.

169. John Wesley Hill, *Abraham Lincoln: Man of God* (1927), 402.

170. 1 John 2:20.

171. D&C 42:45.

172. Matthew 25:21.

173. "Who's on the Lord's Side?" *Hymns,* no. 260.

174. Acts 7:55–60.

175. "Who's on the Lord's Side?" *Hymns,* no. 260.

176. Exodus 3:13–14.

177. Exodus 3:6; emphasis added.

178. Jacob 7:26.

179. Luke 15:17.

180. 2 Nephi 1:23.

181. Alma 32:8, 13.

182. Alma 32:14, 16; emphasis added.

183. Isaiah 49:16; 1 Nephi 21:16.

184. Mosiah 1:5.

185. See D&C 84:95.

186. Amos 8:11.

187. 2 Nephi 32:3.

188. 1 Nephi 1:12.

189. Percy Bysshe Shelley, "Ozymandias," in *New Oxford Book of English Verse,* 580.

190. See 1 Corinthians 12:12–27.

191. Moses 7:18.

192. See John 17.

193. Acts 4:32.

194. See D&C 38:27.

195. D&C 38:2, 7.

196. Mosiah 18:9.

197. Matthew 5:38; see also Leviticus 24:20.

198. 1 Peter 2:23.

199. Ephesians 2:20.

SECTION 2
THE MESSIAH

200. Galatians 3:24.

201. Luke 24:27.

202. Luke 24:44–45; emphasis added.

203. In that same regard, Psalms 146 through 150 are traditionally seen as a conclusion to the full collection of Psalms.

204. Matthew 22:15.

205. Matthew 27:1.

206. Matthew 27:7.

207. See Acts 13:33.

208. Matthew 21:16.

209. Moses 7:35.

210. See 1 Corinthians 15:27; Hebrews 2:6–8.

211. Romans 8:16–17; emphasis added.

212. Acts 2:22–27, 29–32; emphasis added.

213. Acts 13:32–37; emphasis added.

214. See Psalm 16:1.

215. See Psalm 16:5.

216. See Psalm 16:6–7.

217. See Psalm 16:8.

218. Psalm 16:9.

219. See Acts 2:34.

220. Psalm 16:11.

221. D&C 121:36, 46.

222. Hebrews 1:9.

223. 2 Nephi 2:25.

224. For a useful discussion of the names for "God" in the psalms specifically and the Old Testament generally, see Richard P. Belcher, Jr., *The Messiah and Psalms* (2006), especially pages 8, 159.

225. James 1:27.

226. Ephesians 4:8–9; see also D&C 122:8–9.

227. See Psalm 72:20.

228. See Matthew 1:1.

229. Isaiah 61:1.

230. Luke 4:18, 21.

231. Luke 4:29–30.

232. See Matthew 26:64; Mark 16:19; Acts 2:33; 7:55; and 1 Peter 3:22 for just five of the sixteen examples of this "right hand" relationship noted in the scriptures.

233. See Hebrews 5:6; 7:17.

234. See Alma 13:14–19.

235. Alma 13:19.

236. D&C 107:1–5; emphasis in original.

237. Isaiah 8:11, 13–16; 28:16.

238. Acts 4:7–12.

239. 1 Peter 2:4–8.

240. Matthew 21:42–46.

241. Moses 7:53.

242. Matthew 7:24–27.

243. John 13:18, 27, 30; emphasis added.

244. Psalm 35:19.

245. John 15:23–25; emphasis added.

246. Matthew 26:63–64; emphasis added.

247. Matthew 27:34; emphasis added.

248. John 19:23–24; emphasis added.

249. Matthew 27:35–36; emphasis added.

250. Matthew 27:39–42, 44; emphasis added.

251. Matthew 27:45–46; emphasis added.

252. John 19:28–29; emphasis added.

253. Luke 23:44–46; emphasis added.

254. John 19:31–36; emphasis added.

255. Psalm 69:20.

256. James E. Talmage, *Jesus the Christ* (1983 ed.), 620, n. 8.

257. Psalm 22:14. For further documentation of this medical issue, see "On the Physical Death of Jesus Christ," *Journal of the American Medical Association,* March 21, 1986, 1455.

258. 3 Nephi 9:15, 18–21; emphasis added.

259. D&C 59:3–4, 8; emphasis added.

260. Psalms 51:10–11, 16–17; 34:18; emphasis added.

SECTION 3
THE TWENTY-THIRD PSALM

261. Kushner, *The Lord Is My Shepherd*, 9.

262. See Moses 5:5–8, 17–33.

263. Isaiah 53:6.

264. Psalm 95:7.

265. Mosiah 18:9.

266. Isaiah 40:11.

267. Ezekiel 34:11–16.

268. John 10:11–15.

269. Hebrews 13:20.

270. D&C 1:38.

271. Alma 37:16–17.

272. Articles of Faith 1:13.

273. Matthew 5:6.

274. Matthew 6:19.

275. 2 Nephi 9:51.

276. W. Phillip Keller, *A Shepherd Looks at Psalm 23* (1970), 41–42.

277. John 3:5.

278. John 4:14.

279. Kushner, *The Lord Is My Shepherd*, 65.

280. John 4:14.

281. John 6:35, 33.

282. Keller, *A Shepherd Looks at Psalm 23*, 70.

283. 1 Corinthians 10:12.

284. John 15:2.

285. Mosiah 3:19.

286. John 14:6.

287. 2 Nephi 4:32–33.

288. 2 Nephi 31:21; emphasis added.

289. Consider, for example, the Lord changing Abram's name to Abraham and Jacob's name to Israel (see Genesis 17:1–5; 32:28; also Isaiah 62:2; Revelation 2:17; 3:12; D&C 130:11).

290. See 3 Nephi 27:7–8.

291. See D&C 20:37.

292. See D&C 20:77.

293. See D&C 107:1–4.

294. Exodus 3:12.

295. "High on the Mountain Top," *Hymns*, no. 5.

296. Psalm 56:9.

297. Isaiah 11:4.

298. Isaiah 55:1–2.

299. 1 Nephi 22:25–26; emphasis added.

300. See Revelation 19:9.

301. Isaiah 61:1–3.

302. Luke 4:21.

303. Luke 7:36–50.

304. "God Be with You Till We Meet Again," *Hymns*, no. 152.

305. Moroni 7:36.

306. Luke 10:37.

307. Acts 10:38.

308. Genesis 2:23.

309. Gordon B. Hinckley, "Why These Temples?" *Ensign*, August 1974, 39–40.

310. 2 Nephi 31:20.

311. Revelation 7:13–15.

312. 2 Corinthians 1:3.

313. Alma 37:36–37.

SCRIPTURE INDEX

GENESIS

1:1, p. 175
2:23, p. 224
7:1–5, p. 215
14:18, p. 184
39:7–12, p. 17

EXODUS

3:6, p. 126
3:12, p. 215
3:13–14, pp. 125–26
20:17, p. 80
23:11, p. 86

LEVITICUS

24:20, p. 147

JOSHUA

4:5–7, p. 104

1 SAMUEL

2:2, p. 44
2:8, pp. 86–87

JOB

27:3–5, p. 94
31:6, p. 94
38:2, pp. 22–23
38:4, pp. 22–23
38:6, pp. 22–23
38:8, pp. 22–23

38:11, pp. 22–23
40:9, p. 23
40:18, p. 23
42:3, p. 23
42:6, p. 23

PSALMS

1, p. 159
1:1, p. 9
1:1–3, pp. 15–17
2, pp. 159–61, 167
3:2–5, pp. 18–19
4:1, pp. 20–21
4:4, pp. 22–24, 27
4:6–7, pp. 25–26
5:1, pp. 27–29
5:11–12, pp. 30–31
6:2–4, pp. 32–34
6:6, pp. 32–34
6:8, pp. 32–34
8, pp. 162–64
8:2, pp. 35–36
8:3–6, pp. 47–50
11:1, pp. 37-38
12:5, p. 86
12:6, pp. 134–36
13:1, p. 33
15:1–3, pp. 39–41
16, pp. 165–68
16:1, p. 167
16:5, p. 167

16:6–7, p. 167
16:8, p. 168
16:9, p. 168
16:11, p. 168
17:3, pp. 39-41
17:8, p. 42
18:2, pp. 43-44
18:28, pp. 134–36
18:30, pp. 43-44
18:36, pp. 45-46
19:1–3, pp. 47-50
19:13, pp. 51-52
20:7, pp. 53-54
21, pp. 169–70
22:4–5, pp. 55-56
22:7–8, p. 194
22:11, p. 4
22:14, p. 197
22:14–15, p. 195
22:16–17, p. 194
22:18, pp. 193–95
23, pp. 201–26
24, p. 9
24:3–4, pp. 57-59
24:3–6, p. 10
24:3–10, p. 10
24:10, p. 10
25:7, pp. 60-61
25:16–18, p. 5
26:1–2, pp. 93-94
26:11, pp. 93-94
27:4–5, pp. 62-63
27:10, pp. 64-65
27:14, pp. 22–24
30:5, pp. 66-68
31:4–5, p. 195
31:12, pp. 69-70
32:7, pp. 71-72
34:7, pp. 73-75
34:13, pp. 39-41
34:18, pp. 69-70, 198
34:20, p. 195
35, p. 193
35:19, p. 193
36:9, pp. 76-77
37:11, p. 10
37:16, pp. 78-81
37:23–24, pp. 82-83
40:10, pp. 84-85

41:1, pp. 86-89
41:9, p. 192
42:5, pp. 66-68
45, pp. 171–72
45:6, p. 172
45:7, p. 172
46:10, pp. 22–24
49:16–17, pp. 78-81
51:10, pp. 57-59, 69-70
51:10–11, p. 198
51:16–17, p. 198
51:17, pp. 69-70
55:16–17, pp. 90-92
56, p. 217
56:9, pp. 12–14, 217
57, pp. 93-94
57:1, pp. 32-34
57:7, p. 93
61:2, pp. 43-44, 95-96
62:6, pp. 43-44
68, pp. 173–75
69:1–3, p. 5
69:3, pp. 97-98
69:4, pp. 192–93
69:14–17, p. 5
69:20, p. 196
69:21, p. 193
71:9, pp. 99-100
71:18, pp. 99-100
72, pp. 176–78, 180
72:20, p. 178
73:3, pp. 78-81
77:10–12, pp. 101-2
78:5–8, pp. 103-5
78:8, p. 104
85:11, pp. 106-7
86:3–6, pp. 108-10
89, pp. 179–80
89:9, pp. 111-12
89:30–34, pp. 113-14
94:9–10, pp. 115-16
94:18–19, pp. 45-46
95:7, p. 205
100:3, pp. 115-16
100:5, pp. 115-16
102, pp. 181–83
103:8–11, pp. 108-10
103:17–18;, pp. 108-10
105:15, pp. 117-18

107:26–31, pp. 5–6
110, pp. 184–86
110:1, p. 193
113:9, pp. 119-120
116:15, pp. 121-22
118, pp. 187–91
118:6, pp. 123-24
118:24, pp. 125-26
119:15, pp. 27–29
119:19, pp. 127-28
119:48, pp. 27–29
119:58, pp. 108-10
119:59–60, pp. 129-30
119:67, pp. 131-32
119:71–72, pp. 131-32
119:94, p. 133
119:99–100, pp. 115-16
119:103, pp. 134–36
119:105, pp. 134–36
119:108, pp. 137–38
126:5, p. 98
127:1, pp. 139–40
127:3–5, pp. 141–42
130:6, pp. 66-68
133:1, pp. 143–44
139:23, pp. 145–46
141:3, pp. 147–48
141:5, p. 149
144:12, pp. 150–51
145:4, pp. 103-5
145:14, pp. 152–53
146:8, pp. 152–53

PROVERBS

14:12, p. 214
16:25, p. 214
17:5, p. 87
28:27, p. 87

ECCLESIASTES

1:5, p. 68

ISAIAH

2:2–3, p. 9
6:16, p. 89
8:11, p. 188
8:13–16, p. 188
11:4, p. 217
22:23, p. 94

28:16, p. 188
30:15, p. 19
40:11, p. 205
40:28–31, pp. 20–21
49:16, p. 133
53:6, p. 204
55:1, p. 31
55:1–2, pp. 218–19
61, p. 182
61:1, p. 182
61:1–3, p. 220
62:2, p. 215

EZEKIEL

34:11–16, p. 206

DANIEL

6:10, p. 91

AMOS

8:11, p. 135

MALACHI

4:2, p. 4

MATTHEW

1:1, p. 178
2:13–23, p. 74
4:11, p. 74
5:1, p. 9
5:5, p. 10
5:6, p. 208
5:8, p. 9
5:38;, p. 147
6:19, p. 208
7:24–27, pp. 190–91
14:23, p. 37
16:19–21, p. 54
19:14, p. 36
19:21, p. 87
20:16, p. 163
21:13, p. 62
21:42–46, p. 190
22:15, p. 160
25:21, p. 122
26:30, p. 72
26:63–64, p. 193
26:64, p. 184
27:1, p. 160

27:7, p. 160
27:34, p. 193
27:35–36, p. 194
27:39–42, p. 194
27:44, p. 194
27:45–46, pp. 194–95
28:2, p. 74

MARK

1:35–37, p. 38
4:37, p. 111
4:38, p. 112
4:39, p. 112
4:40–41, p. 112

LUKE

1:11–38, p. 73
4, p. 182
4:16–21, p. 220
4:18, p. 183
4:21, p. 183
4:30, p. 183
4:42, p. 38
6:11–12, p. 38
7:36–50, pp. 220–21
10:37, p. 223
15:17, p. 129
19:41–44, p. 98
22:43, p. 74
23:44–46, p. 195
24:23, p. 74
24:27, pp. 157–58
24:44–45, pp. 8, 158

JOHN

2:16, p. 62
3, p. 98
3:5, p. 210
4:14, pp. 210, 212
4:35, p. 19
6:31–35, p. 212
10:11–15, p. 206
11:35, p. 98
12:24, p. 70
13:18, p. 192
13:26, p. 192
13:30, p. 192
14:6, pp. 16, 214
15:2, p. 213

15:23–25, p. 193
17, p. 144
19:23–24, p. 194
19:28–29, p. 195
19:31–36, p. 196

ACTS

2, p. 166
2:22–27, pp. 166–67
2:29–32, pp. 166–67
2:33, p. 184
2:34, p. 168
3:4, p. 96
3:6–7, p. 96
4:8–12, p. 189
4:32, p. 144
7:55–60, p. 124
10:38, p. 223
13:32–37, p. 167
13:33, p. 161

ROMANS

3:23, p. 83
8:16–17, p. 164
8:31, p. 14
8:37, p. 14

1 CORINTHIANS

10:12, p. 213
12, p. 116
12:12–27, p. 143
13:13, p. 67
15:27, p. 164
15:40–42, p. 77

2 CORINTHIANS

1:3, p. 226

GALATIANS

3:24, p. 157

EPHESIANS

4:8–9, p. 175
4:29–32, p. 41

HEBREWS

1:8–9, p. 172
2:6–8, p. 164
5:6, p. 185

6:6, p. 52
7:17, p. 185
13:2, p. 74
13:20, p. 206

JAMES

1:27, p. 175
3:2–10, p. 41
3:17, p. 58

1 PETER

2:4–8, pp. 189–90
2:23, p. 147
3:22, p. 184

1 JOHN

2:20, p. 118

REVELATION

2:17, p. 215
3:12, p. 215
7:13–15, p. 225
19:9, p. 219
21:4, p. 34
22:16, p. 68

1 NEPHI

1:12, p. 135
4:2, p. 55
8, p. 16
8:12–13, p. 84
21:16, p. 133
22:25–26, p. 219

2 NEPHI

1:23, p. 129
2:11, p. 4
2:25, pp. 30, 101, 172
4:32–33, p. 214
9:29, p. 116
9:51, p. 208
25:13, p. 4
25:21–27, p. 105
31:20, pp. 101, 225
31:21, p. 215
32:3, p. 135
33:3, p. 34

JACOB

2:17–19, p. 80
7:26, pp. 127–28

ENOS

1:9, p. 84
1:11, p. 84

MOSIAH

1:5, p. 134
3:19, p. 214
4:19, p. 87
4:26, p. 87
16:9, p. 77
18:9, pp. 146, 205
24:14, p. 46
24:15, p. 46

ALMA

1:27, p. 88
4:13, p. 88
5:19, p. 85
5:55, p. 88
8:14–15, p. 19
13:14–19, p. 185
13:19, p. 185
30:44, p. 48
32:8, p. 131
32:13, p. 131
32:14, pp. 131–32
32:16, pp. 131–32
32:23, p. 36
33:3, p. 90
34:21, p. 91
34:27, p. 90
34:28, p. 88
34:38, p. 102
37:16–17, p. 207
37:36, p. 90
37:36–37, p. 226
42:16, p. 101
42:25, p. 13

HELAMAN

5:12, p. 44

3 NEPHI

9:15, pp. 197–98
9:18–21, pp. 197–98

14:20, p. 80
17:21–23, p. 35
18:18, pp. 90, 91
25:2, p. 4
26:14, pp. 35, 36
26:16, p. 35
27:7–8, p. 215

MORMON

8:37, p. 88

MORONI

7: 30, pp. 74–75
7: 35–37, pp. 74–75
7:36, p. 223
7:48, p. 58

DOCTRINE AND COVENANTS

1:38, pp. 114, 207
5:34, p. 23
6:33, p. 98
6:34, p. 44
20:33, p. 90
20:37, p. 215
20:77, p. 215
38:2, p. 146
38:7, p. 146
38:27, p. 144
42:31, p. 88
42:45, p. 121
43:9, pp. 58–59
43:14, pp. 58–59
52:14, p. 91
58:42, p. 61
59:3–4, p. 198
59:8, pp. 70, 198
61:39, p. 90
63:64, pp. 39–40
76:50–112, p. 77

84:46, p. 76
84:95, p. 135
105:3, p. 89
107:1–4, p. 215
107:1–5, pp. 185–86
121:1–3, p. 33
121:2, p. 33
121:3, p. 33
121:7, p. 33
121:9, p. 34
121:10, p. 34
121:36, p. 172
121:46, p. 172
122:8–9, p. 175
123:17, p. 23
128:22–23, p. 107
130:11, p. 215

MOSES

1:33, p. 48
5:5–8, p. 203
5:6–8, p. 73
5:17–33, p. 203
7:18, p. 144
7:28, p. 98
7:29, p. 98
7:32, p. 98
7:35, p. 163
7:37, p. 98
7:53, p. 190
7:61, p. 106
7:62, p. 106

JOSEPH SMITH–HISTORY

1:16, p. 77

ARTICLES OF FAITH

1:4, p. 53
1:13, p. 207

SUBJECT INDEX

Affliction, 131–32. *See also* Trials
Agency, 209
Aging, 99–100
Ally, God as, 123–24
Ancestors, 55–56
Angels, 73–75, 222–23
Anointing, 219–21
Apostles, sustaining, 117–18
Arrogance, 115–16
Atonement: salvation through, 4, 165–68; psalms concerning, 192–98
Augustine, St., 30

Banquet, 218–19
Baptism, 210
Beatitudes, 9–10
Beggar, healing of, 95–96, 189–90
Blessings: gratitude for, 101–2, 222; for righteous women, 119–20; of Jesus Christ, 169–70
Body, 143–44
Bones, breaking, 195–96
Book of Mormon, 107
Bread of life, 212
Broken hearts, 70, 198
Broken things, 69–70

"Cast down" sheep, 212–13
Children: becoming like, 35–36; love of, 42, 64–65; hope for, 83, 150; teaching, 103–5; for righteous women, 119–20; wayward, 141–42

Children of God, 48–50, 133, 141–42, 162–64
Church leaders, sustaining, 117–18
Cicero, 111
Cleanliness, 57–59
Clothing, of Jesus Christ, 193–94
"Come, Come, Ye Saints," 72
"Come, Thou Fount of Every Blessing," 94
"Come unto Him," 50
Comfort, 6–7, 208–9, 217–18
Coming to ourselves, 129–30
Commandments, 15–17, 113–14
Companionship, 215–17
Compassion, 108–10, 114
Consecration, 79
Contrite spirit, 70, 198
Correction, 129–30, 149
Counsel, 149
"Count Your Blessings," 102
Covetousness, 80–81, 207–8
Creations, 47–49
Crucifixion, 192–98. *See also* Atonement
Crying, 34, 97–98

Darkness, 67–68, 76
Daughters, 150–51
David, 117, 176–78
Death, 121–22, 165–68, 196–97
Desires, 207–8
Despair, 32–34
Divine nature, 48–50, 162–64
Donne, John, 30–31

Earth: as sign, 47–48; as home, 127–28
Elohim, 175
Emerson, Ralph Waldo, 99
Enduring, 20–21, 33, 97–98
Enemies, 192–93, 218–19
Enoch, 97–98
Envy, 80–81, 207–8
Eternal families, 224–25
Evil, 91, 215–17
Exaltation, 33–34
Example, sharing gospel through, 85

Faith: in Jesus Christ, 53–54; through
    trials, 111–12; in God, 113–14
Family, 141–42, 224–25
Fatigue, 211–13
Fear, 67–68, 208–9, 215–17
Finances, 78–81
Fixing hearts, 93–94
Foolish people, 80
Forebears, 55–56
Forgetting past sins, 61
Forgiveness: for youth, 60–61; possibility
    of, 82–83, 109–10
Foundation, God as, 43–44
Freewill offering, of mouth, 137–38
Friends, 34
Funerals, 121
Future, 125

Generations, teaching future, 103–5
Getting away, 37–38
God: love of, 12–14, 42, 65, 152–53;
    obedience to, 15–17; help from, 18–19,
    45–46, 139–40, 213–15; standing in
    awe of, 22–24; trust in, 30–31; as rock,
    43–44; light surrounding, 77; weeps for
    His children, 97–98; teaching children
    about, 103–5; nature of, 108–10; faith
    in, 113–14; as ally, 123–24; constancy
    of, 125–26; turning toward, 129–30;
    understanding, 134; interview with,
    145–46; challenges of, 160; Christ's
    relationship with, 184; companionship
    of, 215–17; goodness and mercy of,
    222–24. See also Children of God
Golden Psalm, 165–68
Good, recognizing, 25–26
Goodness, 222–24
Gospel: sharing, 84–85; restoration of,
    106–7

Gratitude, 101–2, 222
"Great transgression," 51–52
Green pastures, 208–9
Guardian angels, 223
Guidance, 213–15

Happiness: through trust in God, 30–31;
    sharing gospel through, 85; tears and,
    98; remembering, 101–2; promises of,
    172
Harmony, 143–44
Hart, A. W. "Mickey," 57
Healing, of lame man, 95–96, 189–90
Heart: broken, 70, 198; fixing, 93–94
Help, divine, 45–46, 139–40, 213–15,
    222–23
Higher ground, 95–96
Hinckley, Gordon B., 224–25
Holy Ghost, and meditation, 28–29
Home, 127–28
Hope, 66–68
House of Lord, 224–25
Humility, 57–59, 116, 131–32, 149
Hymns, 71–72

Illness, 143
Integrity, 94
Intelligence, pride in, 115–16
Interviews, 145–46

Jacob, 127–28
JAH, 173–75. See also Jehovah
Jehovah, 173–75, 225–26
Jesus Christ: salvation through, 4, 165–68;
    psalms and, 7–8, 157–58, 192–98;
    appears to Nephites, 35–36; solitude
    and, 37–38; as Rock, 44, 187–91;
    faith in, 53–54; second coming of, 68;
    angels watch over, 73–74; as light, 77;
    light surrounding, 77; weeps for His
    people, 98; calms storm, 111–12; plan
    of salvation and, 160–61; as Son of
    Man, 163–64; blessings of, 169–70;
    description of, 171–72; Solomon and,
    176–78; reign of, 179–82; as Messiah,
    182–83; Melchizedek and, 184–86;
    as Shepherd, 204–6; as bread of life,
    212; as guide, 213–15; companionship
    of, 215–17; goodness and mercy of,
    223–24. See also Messiah
Job, 22–23, 94

Joy. *See* Happiness
Judas, 192

Keller, Phillip, 212
Kindness, in speech, 39–41
Kings, 169–70
Knowledge, pride in, 115–16
Kushner, Harold S., 202–3, 211

Lame man, healing of, 95–96, 189–90
Law, divine, 15–17
Lee, Harold B., 96
Lewis, C. S., 49
Light of Christ, 76–77
Lincoln, Abraham, 118
Loneliness, 127–28
Love: of God, 12–14, 42, 65, 152–53; for
  children, 64–65
Luther, Martin, 93

Maketh, 209
Marriage, for righteous women, 119–20
Materialism, 53–54
McKay, David O., 28
Meditation, 27–29, 102
Melchizedek, 184–86
Mercy, 108–10, 114, 222–24
Messiah: salvation through, 4; description
  of, 171–72; Jesus Christ as, 182–83;
  Melchizedek and, 184–86; prophecy
  on, 220. *See also* Jesus Christ
Millennium, 181–82
Missionary work, 84–85
Money, 78–81
Mortality: trials as part of, 3–7; as home,
  127–28
Moses, 125–26
Mouth, freewill offering of, 137–38
Music, 71–72

Name, of Jesus Christ, 215
Natural man, 213–14
Needs, 206–7
Nephites, Jesus appears to, 35–36
New Testament, Old Testament and, 7–8,
  57–58

Obedience, 15–17, 113–14
Old age, 99–100

Old Testament, New Testament and, 7–8,
  57–58
Ordinances, 224–25
"Ozymandias" (Shelley), 139–40

Packer, Boyd K., 118
Paine, Thomas, 6
Parenthood, 64–65, 83, 103–5, 141–42
Past, 125
Patience, 23–24, 32–34
Peace, 27–29, 143–44, 208–9
Peter, heals lame man, 95–96, 189–90
Plan of salvation, 3–4, 160–61
Pope, Alexander, 80
Poverty/Poor, 79, 86–89
Prayer: psalms as, 6–7; answers to, 18;
  meditation and, 28–29; call to, 90–92
Present, 125–26
Presumptuous sins, 51–52
Pride, 115–16
Priesthood: restoration of, 107; promises
  of, 172
Prodigal son, 129
Progress, through trials, 3–4, 20–21
Prophets, sustaining, 117–18
Provident living, 79–80
Psalm 23: overview of, 201–4; "The Lord is
  my shepherd," 204–6; "I shall not want,"
  206–8; "He maketh me to lie down in
  green pastures," 208–9; "He leadeth
  me beside the still waters," 210–11; "He
  restoreth my soul," 211–13; "He leadeth
  me in the paths of righteousness for his
  name's sake," 213–15; "I will fear no evil:
  for thou art with me," 215–17; "Thy rod
  and thy staff, they comfort me," 217–18;
  "Thou preparest a table before me in
  the presence of mine enemies," 218–19;
  "Thou anointest my head with oil; my
  cup runneth over," 219–22; "Surely
  goodness and mercy shall follow me,"
  222–24; "I will dwell in the house of the
  Lord for ever," 224–25
Psalm of the Precious Secret, 165–68
Psalms, purposes of, 6–7
Purity, 57–59

Quiet, 27–29

Rebellion, 159–61
Record-keeping, 103–5

Renewal, 211–13
Repentance: of youth, 60–61; possibility of, 82–83
Reproof, 149
Rest, 211–13
Restoration, 106–7
Resurrection, 166–68
Revelation, continuing, 15, 136
Riches, 78–81
Righteousness, 153, 213–15, 219
Rock, 43–44, 187–91
Rod, 217–18

Sabbath, 211
Sacrifice, 69–70, 135, 169–70, 197–98
Salvation: through Atonement, 4, 165–68; God desires our, 12–13
Satan, 129–30
Saul, 117
Scriptures, 134–36
Second Coming, 68
Self-correction, 129–30
Self-pity, 34
Sermon on the Mount, 9–10
Sheep, 203, 204–6, 208, 212–13
Shelley, Percy Bysshe, 139–40
Shepherd(s), 203, 204–6, 217–18
Signs, 47–48
Silence, 147–48
Sin(s): presumptuous, 51–52; of youth, 60–61; repentance from, 82–83
Sleep, 19
Smith, Hyrum, 135
Smith, Joseph: in Liberty Jail, 33; friends of, 34; on Restoration, 107; sacrifice of, 135
Solitude, 37–38
Solomon, 176–78
"Son of man," 163–64
Speech, 39–41, 137–38, 147–48
Spirit: contrite, 70, 198; music's influence on, 71
Staff, 217–18
Standing still, 23–24
Stars, 48
Steadfastness, 93–94
Stephen, 124
Still, standing, 23–24
Still waters, 210–11
Stone, 43–44, 187–91
Storm, Jesus calms, 111–12

Strength, through trials, 20–21
"Sweet Hour of Prayer," 92

Talmage, James E., 197
Tears, 34, 97–98
Temple: purity and, 57–59; as holy place, 62–63; as house of Lord, 224–25
Temple psalms, 8–10
Temptation, 91
Testimony, sharing, 105
Thompson, Francis, 222
Tongues, bridling, 39–41. See also Speech
Transgression, 51–52. See also Sin(s)
Trials: as part of mortality, 3–7; causes of, 16, 33; help through, 18–19, 45–46; strength through, 20–21, 191; patience through, 22–24; seeking good during, 25–26; enduring, 32–34, 97–98; of forebears, 55–56; temple and, 62–63; hope through, 66–68; of aging, 99–100; faith through, 111–12; humility through, 131–32; righteousness through, 153
Trouble, choosing, 16–17
Trust, in God, 30–31
Twenty-third Psalm. See Psalm 23

Unity, 143–44

Vain/Vanity, 115–16, 160
Valleys, 215–16

Want, 206–8
Water, 210–11
Waves, Jesus calms, 111–12
Wayward children, 141–42
Weeping, 34, 97–98
"Who's on the Lord's Side?" 123, 124
Wicked, 80
Women: blessings for righteous, 119–20; as gems, 150–51
Words, 39–41, 137–38, 147–48
Wrongs, responding to, 147–48

Yahweh or "yhwh," 173–75. See also Jehovah
Youth, repentance and, 60–61

Zion, 181–82
Zoramites, 131–32